TABLE OF CONTENTS

HAMILTON
ONE SHOT TO BROADWAY

THE UNOFFICIAL STORY OF THE HIT MUSICAL

Edited by Caleb Casey

SYMETTRICA
PUBLISHING

INTRODUCTION

What can be said about *Hamilton*? Two words: a phenomenon. When *Hamilton* first premiered in February 2015, it was an instant hit. Universally acclaimed by critics, the play soon became the hottest ticket in New York City, with queues for the chance to get a seat stretching around the block. The unlikely mix of history, hip-hop and musical theater caught almost everyone by surprise, nothing quite like it had ever been seen on Broadway before.

The music, staging and energy of the show brought a new, youthful feel to musical theater, which had stagnated somewhat since the turn of the millennium, while the multi-ethnic casting felt like a reflection of contemporary America in the Obama era. It reached audiences that perhaps hadn't always felt welcomed by Broadway: young people, people of color; these constituencies became part of the legions of fans that made *Hamilton* the talk of the nation, the show that everyone *had* to see.

Hamilton broke out of New York within a year, opening at the CIBC Theater in Chicago in 2016 and hitting the road shortly thereafter. A travelling production that sang and danced its way through the cities of North America, tickets sold out within twenty-four hours of going on sale, hundreds of thousands of people queuing online, breathlessly refreshing their browsers for a chance to get one.

An international production opened at the Victoria Palace Theatre, London, in 2017, put together by the legendary musical impresario Sir Cameron Mackintosh, who had been responsible for bringing to the stage *Les Misérables, Oliver!, The Phantom of the Opera* and *Cats*, among many other internationally famous shows. Further productions

◀ *Lin-Manuel Miranda*

opened in Sydney, Australia, and Hamburg, Germany, followed by an international tour as the *Hamilton* phenomenon went global.

And it wasn't just audiences who were captivated by the show, the critical response was sensational. Ben Brantley, writing in *The New York Times* said, "I am loath to tell people to mortgage their houses and lease their children to acquire tickets to a hit Broadway show. But *Hamilton* might just about be worth it". David Cote of *Time Out* said, "I love *Hamilton*. I love it like I love New York, or Broadway when it gets it right. And this is so right... the work's human drama and novelistic density remain astonishing."

Hamilton was showered with awards: eleven Tony Awards, including Best Musical, Best Score and Best Actor; seven Laurence Olivier Awards, including Best New Musical; the Grammy for Best Musical Theater album, and the Pulitzer Prize for Drama. It was a level of success that made an instant star of the show's young creator, Lin-Manuel Miranda, then a thirty-five-year-old New Yorker of Puerto Rican descent, who had become captivated by the story of Alexander Hamilton, one of the more obscure Founding Fathers, and decided to tell that story through the medium of hip-hop.

Miranda's singular vision brought the sounds, and faces, of 21st Century America to a re-telling of his nation's history at a pivotal moment in that history, as the first African-American President of the United States concluded his term in office. It was a context in which Miranda's casting of Christopher Jackson to play a black George Washington felt powerfully symbolic, a statement that American history belonged to *all* the people of the modern, diverse nation that the United States had become.

Over the intervening years, Lin-Manuel Miranda has matured into something of a national treasure, a charismatic, multi-talented star of stage and screen celebrated for his work with Disney, in particular, a partnership that has seen Miranda contribute music for *Moana*, *Encanto* and *Star Wars*, take a leading role in *Mary Poppins Returns* and produce a filmed version of *Hamilton* that streamed on Disney+ in 2020.

It is the screen that has recently become the focus of Lin-Manuel's efforts, and he made his directorial debut in 2021 with *Tick, Tick... Boom!*, a biopic that explored the life and work of *Rent* creator Jonathan Larson. It's notable, though, that the subject of the film remains the stage, the location of Miranda's original passion, and the play that catapulted him to global superstardom.

This book brings together reflections from cast, crew, critics, commentators and historians to tell the story of *Hamilton*: the phenomenon, the music, the history, and the man whose outstanding talent made it all happen.

THE COMMENTATORS

ANTHONY DECURTIS

Anthony DeCurtis is a distinguished author, journalist, and academic, renowned for his contributions to music criticism and cultural commentary. A longtime contributing editor at *Rolling Stone*, he has written extensively about music history.

DeCurtis holds a PhD in American literature from Indiana University and serves as a Distinguished Lecturer in the Creative Writing Program at the University of Pennsylvania, where he teaches courses on arts, culture, and music writing. His published works include *Lou Reed: A Life* (2017), a critically acclaimed biography, and, with Clive Davis, *The Soundtrack of My Life* (2013). He is also a Grammy Award winner for his album notes to Eric Clapton's *Crossroads* box set.

Anthony's unique ability to blend academic insight with journalistic flair has established him as a leading voice in music criticism.

JESSE GREEN

Jesse Green is the chief theater critic for *The New York Times*, a position he has held since 2017. Prior to joining the *Times*, he served as theater critic and contributing editor for *New York Magazine*. Green's award-winning career spans decades, during which he has written extensively on theater and culture more broadly.

In addition to journalism, Green has authored several books, including *The Velveteen Father* (1999), and, with Mary Rodgers, *Shy: The Alarmingly Outspoken Memoirs of Mary Rodgers* (2022), co-written. The latter was celebrated as one of *The New York Times'* "100 Notable Books of 2022."

JIM KEILY

Jim Keily is a history professor at East Los Angeles College, who has also had a long and successful career as a writer for television. He has been involved in the creation and production of various shows, including *Lucky, Normal, Ohio,* and *Raising Dad.* His dual expertise in storytelling and history reflects his commitment to creative and educational pursuits.

JASON KING

Jason King is a Canadian-American music scholar, journalist, musician, and educator, known for his multidisciplinary expertise in music and cultural studies.

King has made significant contributions to music education and scholarship. He was a founding faculty member at the Clive Davis Institute of Recorded Music at NYU's Tisch School of the Arts, where he held various leadership roles, including Chair and Artistic Director. In 2023, he became the Dean of the USC Thornton School of Music, where he continues to shape music education, emphasizing interdisciplinary approaches and a comprehensive understanding of the music industry.

An inaugural member of the Hip-Hop Culture Council at the Kennedy Center and the *Black Genius Brain Trust* advocacy group for black artists, King has also served on the editorial board of the *Journal of Popular Music Studies.* His career spans music production, songwriting, performance, and extensive journalistic and academic writing on topics such as African Diasporic cultural studies, music business, and gender studies.

BIRTE PFLEGER

Birte Pfleger is a historian specializing in early American history, immigration, and ethnicity, particularly in the context of German-American communities. She earned her Ph.D. from the University of California, Irvine, and has been a professor of history at California State University, Los Angeles, since 2003.

Michael Riedel

Michael Riedel is a prominent American theater critic, journalist, and author known for his sharp wit and deep insights into Broadway and the theater world. Riedel is best known for his long-running column in the *New York Post*, where he has covered the Broadway scene with a mix of biting commentary, behind-the-scenes scoops, and informed critiques. His column became a must-read for theater insiders and enthusiasts alike, with his sometime polarizing style making him both an influential and controversial figure in the industry.

In addition to his journalistic work, Riedel has authored two books about Broadway: *Razzle Dazzle: The Battle for Broadway* (2015), which delves into the history and revival of the Great White Way, and *Singular Sensation: The Triumph of Broadway* (2020), which chronicles the evolution of Broadway in the 1990s.

Riedel is also a frequent guest and commentator on television and radio, where he contributes to discussions about theater and the arts.

Jayson Rodriguez

Jayson Rodriguez is a seasoned music journalist, creative consultant, and executive producer with over 20 years of experience in hip-hop and R&B coverage. He has written for *MTV News*, *XXL*, *Rolling Stone*, and *Billboard* among many other, conducting interviews with major artists including Jay-Z and Kanye West.

In addition to writing, Rodriguez has produced content for outlets like Revolt TV and Vevo and worked on *The Bridge*, a podcast celebrating 50 years of hip-hop. He is also the creator of the acclaimed newsletter *Backseat Freestyle*, which explores hip-hop's cultural and artistic dimensions.

And the cast & crew of *Hamilton*

▲   *In The Heights*

1. BORN IN THE HEIGHTS

Lin-Manuel Miranda was born on January the 16th, 1980 in the heavily Latino neighbourhood of New York City known as Washington Heights. His father, Luis, and mother, Luz, were both of Puerto Rican origin, Luis having moved to New York in the early 1970s to pursue an education and the opportunities that life in the Big Apple might present.

Luis soon embarked on a spectacularly successful political career, becoming an advisor to the Democratic mayor of New York City, Ed Koch, and going on to be appointed Director of the Mayor's Office for Hispanic Affairs. He would later work for Rudolph Giuliani, Hilary Clinton, Chuck Schumer and Letitia James. It was a career that bought the Miranda family a comfortable life in Inwood, just north of Washington Heights in Upper Manhattan, where a young Lin-Manual showed a precocious talent for music, a talent that would earn him a place at Wesleyan University in the late nineties.

Jesse Green: Lin-Manuel Miranda is basically a renaissance man of musical theater. He went to Wesleyan, which is a good liberal arts school, and it was at that time that he began to merge a lot of his interests from his youth growing up in New York, in musical theater, in hip-hop; developing hip-hop, salsa and other kinds of Latino music and all kinds of sounds and ideas that sort of intersected in his personality. And starting in college, he began to use those to forge musical theater of his own that would, in the end, come to form a kind of basis for a revolution in what musical theater could be.

During his time at Wesleyan, Lin-Manuel sought out like-minded collaborators, with whom he formed a hip-hop comedy troupe called *Freestyle Love Supreme*.

Jesse Green: They would essentially write instantaneous theater songs with a hip-hop quality. I happened to catch him doing that with Chris Jackson, who ended up playing George Washington in *Hamilton*, at a very small theater called Ars Nova. And it was pretty clear that there was some astonishing talent going on. What made it astonishing wasn't just the speed, we're getting used to people delivering lyrics at a fast speed these days, it was a little new then, but the fact that it was improvised. The rhymes, the complexity of the thinking spat out at fifty words a minute was kind of overwhelming, and I thought at the time, "well, that is amazing, but what on earth can he do with that?" I thought it was kind of a dead end, frankly, I didn't see where that could go. Then we get *In The Heights*.

It was during his sophomore year at Wesleyan that Lin-Manuel's prodigious talent started to separate him from his peers. He began writing the first draft of *In The Heights*, a musical with an unusual blend of Latin music, salsa and elements of rap that was set in the Dominican-American neighbourhood of his birth and followed the fortunes of various characters within the community. The project piqued the interest of some of the older students at Wesleyan, including the aspiring director Thomas Kail. Together with Kail and the playwright Quiara Alegría Hudes, Lin-Manuel expanded *In The Heights* into a full production, which premiered to a small audience at the Eugene O'Neill Theater Center in Waterford, Connecticut in the summer of 2005.

Lin-Manuel Miranda: I loved musicals, I wanted a life in musicals. I knew I was never going to get cast as "Bernardo" because I'm not a ballet dancer. I knew I would never be cast in *Man of La Mancha* because I have a rock voice, I don't have an operatic voice. And if you want to be in musicals, and you're a Puerto Rican dude, that's really all you got, that was what

▲ *Lin-Manuel Miranda*

existed in the canon. So I started writing *In The Heights* because I wanted to make a way for myself.

Jesse Green: *In The Heights* began as a college project in 1999, when he would have been nineteen, and was developed in various ways and with various people over a period of almost ten years. It was done in workshops and readings, and then it was done off-Broadway, and then it was moved to Broadway in 2008. *In The Heights* is a very traditional musical, using a non-traditional musical idiom, by which I mean in terms of the story and the structure and the way character is developed in it and the kinds of characters in it, it would have been familiar to an Oscar Hammerstein. That's not a putdown, that's a compliment. But what made it distinct from that tradition was that it was using different sounds than had formerly been used in musical storytelling on Broadway. It merged hip-hop and Latin music, in addition to traditional theater music. And all of these threads are kind of woven through it while telling a very traditional story that anyone who had been to musicals in the past fifty years would recognise and not be thrown by.

Jason King: I saw *In The Heights* on Broadway, and I remember being very, very impressed by it. Lin-Manuel, for those who haven't experienced his talent, is somebody who is extraordinarily gifted. As an actor, he's incredibly generous, as a wordsmith, I think that's really where a lot of his power lies. He just writes these rhymes that are so clever, so thoughtful, so well-constructed that they dazzle. You saw that in *In The Heights* in the opening number alone, it just took your breath away that he was able to paint this entire picture of life in Washington Heights and the Dominican-American community. It's him basically introducing us to all of these characters who are in the Heights, who are part of the narrative of the musical, and he's like your tour guide through the neighbourhood. The language, the excitement of it, *In The Heights* on Broadway was just a really exciting cultural moment, it was really powerful. And I think a lot of that is rooted in Lin-Manuel's skill as a lyricist and as a composer.

Michael Riedel: The thing you have to understand about Lin is that, while he loves hip-hop and he loves rap music, he's fundamentally steeped in musical theater. He knows the music of Richard Rodgers and Cole Porter and Stephen Sondheim, and that allows him to then go to the hip-hop world, go to the rap world, but still understand that those songs have to function as theatrical songs, as musical theater songs. He understands musical theater where hip-hop artists have failed on Broadway in the past, if they don't understand that hip-hop can tell a story, if it's just a cascade of words making political points.

Lin understands that a musical works because the songs are an expression of the character, what the character's feeling, what the character's thinking, what the character wants. He understands that's how you make a musical, so his rap and hip-hop songs drive the character and the narrative forward. He also has the ability to then take a break from that cascade of hip-hop rapping words and give you an old-fashioned, beautiful Broadway ballad, so he integrates contemporary music with an old-world style of Broadway that I think still has currency.

Jesse Green: One of the things that comes through in *In The Heights*, that is definitely from him, and not merely a reflection of the ethnic composition of the cast or the creatives, is the joy of the central character, "Usnavi", who is living in Washington Heights, which is where Miranda was born. The joy of that character seemed to me, and to I think most critics or anyone who knew him, to be a very direct expression of the joy that Lin-Manuel Miranda himself brought to the theater. The incredible charisma of Lin-Manuel Miranda, that was the first time we had seen that coming through full bore in a musical written by the person who was playing it. It's important to note that both in *In The Heights* and especially in *Hamilton*, a lot of it was written by the author for himself to perform, knowing what he can do. Is that rare? It is extremely rare. You have to go back to Noel Coward, George M. Cohan, there's a few people who have written both music and lyrics, not very many, but a few, famously Stephen Sondheim. There's a few who have written music, lyrics, and the book of a show, but adding in the writing of the entire show, plus performing in it, I can only really think of Noel Coward and George M. Cohan.

Michael Riedel: We haven't had a lot of Latino shows on Broadway. I mean, I think of *West Side Story* and *In The Heights*, and that's pretty much the extent of it. And Lin is a New York City kid, and a lot of Broadway shows tended to be set either in the past or in a kind of fantasy world, the fantasy world of *The Lion King* or the 19th century opera house of *The Phantom of the Opera*. Lin's show was contemporary, it was his life in the Heights, the people in his neighbourhood, it was contemporary and it was infectious. I was not particularly fond of it, it seemed a sort of a sappy, sentimental view of Latino culture up in Washington Heights, where everybody seemed to be happy and having a good time and bouncing around. There was a far better musical called *Passing Strange*, which was much tougher and grittier, more to my tastes. So, frankly, I didn't think very much about Lin-Manuel Miranda, but he did have a kind of buoyancy and an infectious energy about not only a show, but also about his personality.

Jayson Rodriguez: I think *In The Heights* kind of established him as the new Spike Lee. It's a brilliant piece of writing. And on a surface level, you think it's a story about striving, which it is, and also family and cultural diversity, where you see this Latin family in the Heights. But, really, it's a story about gentrification, that's sort of like the Trojan horse that gets into this deeper topic, there is this fear of change as the current that runs through the production. And it's not just generational change, it's the change of this neighbourhood, and so in the same way that Spike Lee has made something like a *Jungle Fever* that people thought that was about interracial love, but it was really about drug addiction, *In The Heights* isn't necessarily this quaint family tale, it's really a tale about gentrification in Manhattan.

There has been a historical absence of Latino and Hispanic representation, not just in theater, but in American arts generally. *In The Heights* represented a chance to showcase not only Lin-Manuel

Miranda's talent, but the wide pool of underused talent within Latino communities. Around the time of the play's release, Lin collaborated with the actor Antonio Banderas on a project to help promote Latino voices in theater and the arts and to expand opportunities within his community.

Jayson Rodriguez: There's been a dearth of Latino participation in the arts, particularly with plays and Broadway. It's just something systemically that's happening in our country where there's a lack of resources that are provided to schools and certain neighbourhoods.

Jason King: There's definitely been an absence of Latino voices in the theater in particular, Broadway has often been known as the "Great White Way", and that term is both a metaphor, but also based in reality. It has long been an institution in American life that has either caricatured people of color or marginalised them, and it has not been a space for people of color to demonstrate their full humanity and all of the aspects of what it means to be a person of color in this country. I think Latinos have often had to struggle for representation in the theater, so while we can look to fantastic moments of Latino representation like *A Chorus Line* in the mid 1970s, it's been a struggle, and I think Lin-Manuel has been incredibly transformative in terms of making a case for Latinos to be included in the American theater scene.

In The Heights proved to be a spectacular success, and established Miranda as a major new voice in musical theater. The play was nominated for a total of thirteen Tony awards, winning for Best Musical, Best Original Score, Best Choreography and Best Orchestrations as well as picking up a Grammy award for Best Musical and a nomination for the Pulitzer Prize for Drama.

Jason King: *In The Heights* was successful because it's a really well-done show. It has a great book, the characters are wonderful and appealing and heartening. Lin-Manuel was in it and he's a just galvanising human being and artist, so he brought a lot of visibility just based on the power of his own acting and rhyming in the show. But I think it was also successful because it was announcing a new moment in American theatre, in which a show starring people of color, by people of color, could be prominent, could win awards in a way that challenged the narrative of the Broadway as the "Great White way", and in which these traditionally marginalised voices could actually come to the centre of culture and be represented.

Jesse Green: New York audiences enjoy (I don't mean this negatively) being flattered by the idea that we've come really far and that we are ready to accept each new wave of people who claw their way up and try to get into the cultural arena. By the time of *In The Heights*, I think people were happy to congratulate themselves on more inclusivity and diversity in the theater. That is not the only reason it was a hit. It's also very successfully did what it set out to do, but if it weren't for the fact that it also flattered the political hopes of the core audience, I don't think it would have won so many awards.

Jayson Rodgriguez: Part of it, is it was different, right? Different attracts attention. It's brilliant as a piece of pop art, but then it has something deeper and substantial to it that you can wrap your brain around. That's really the thing that win awards, right? Where it's good for you, but it's fun for you at the same time.

Jason King: It's rare to see an original musical where somebody writes the lyrics and the music and the actual script itself, as well as the score, but even more rare to see a largely Latino and

African-American cast performing a musical on Broadway. It was a great moment to see somebody who had incorporated sounds like salsa music and hip-hop into a musical, get that kind of visibility and success. I don't know how often we'll ever see somebody like Lin-Manuel Miranda and the talent that he represents.

Michael Riedel: I have to give him credit here: he was one of the very first Broadway people to understand the importance of social media. He was tweeting up a storm and Facebooking up a storm with *In The Heights* and it was just at a time when Twitter was taking off and he fundamentally understood that that was a new way to talk about your Broadway show. He understood that the audience for Broadway was changing, it was no longer for what we used to call "the blue-haired matinee ladies". It used to be for your grandmother, not anymore. Not since *Rent*, not since *Chicago*, not since *Wicked*, which were very popular with young people who, of course, are adept at social media. Lin understood that. And he amassed a huge audience for his next show after *In The Heights*, which turned out to be *Hamilton*.

2. HIS NAME IS ALEXANDER HAMILTON

L in-Manuel Miranda and Alexander Hamilton first met in 2008, while Lin was in the first flush of his spectacular success with *In The Heights*. Lin had departed to Mexico on vacation, taking with him the celebrated historian Ron Chernow's voluminous, 2004 biography of Hamilton: it proved to be a life-changing event. One of the more obscure Founding Fathers of the United States, few Americans would have heard of Hamilton, other than that his face appears on the ten-dollar bill, but Miranda was fascinated by his story and begun to imagine a new project: a musical based around the life of this little known, eighteenth-century politician.

Jason King: I think it's kind of surprising that Lin-Manuel decided to do an entire musical based on the life of Alexander Hamilton, especially having done *In The Heights* previously. I don't know if you read the biography of Alexander Hamilton and just think, "wow, this would make a really good hip-hop musical". It's a curious choice of source material, but yet at the same time it's clear that Lin-Manuel saw elements in the biography of Alexander Hamilton that he could use to craft a story about the nature of the American character and the American dream.

If you spoke to most people on the street, I don't know that they would know who Alexander Hamilton is, other than the fact that he might have been involved in some way in the Constitution, that he was one of the Founding Fathers.

◀ *Alexander Hamilton, 1792*

23

▲ *Alexander Hamilton*

I don't know much about his background, about his history, about where he comes from, and certainly don't think of him in any way in relationship to hip-hop at all. So, it was a really bold choice of Lin-Manuel to choose Alexander Hamilton as a subject, but also an interesting one because he could really fill in the gaps in people's knowledge and deliver to them a subject who is important to American history, but a little bit forgotten.

Alexander Hamilton's early life took place during the most critical period in American history. The Revolutionary War broke out while he was still a student, and the young Hamilton played an active role in the turbulent politics of the time, eventually rising to become one of the most important figures in the birth of American Independence.

Birte Pfleger: Alexander Hamilton was probably the most important person of the American Revolution who was not President. He started writing in support of the revolution when he was just a young student at Columbia, he was very active in the military, he became a close confidant of George Washington, he was at the Constitutional Convention, he was instrumental in getting New York to ratify the Constitution, and, of course, a major author of The Federalist Papers. He became the first Secretary of the Treasury, putting the United States on a really sound financial footing, even though his personal life was not on a sound financial footing.

Jim Keily: What Lin-Manuel seems to focus on, through hip-hop of course, is the story of a self-made man, somebody young and hungry. He comes over to the United States to start a new life and ends up rising to heights that he himself could never have guessed, and I think that that's the aspirational impact and drive of the entire play. I think that's what people relate to. Whenever you do any kind of story, there's an underdog who's trying to achieve, and that's certainly the appeal of Hamilton, who achieved far beyond anything he could have imagined himself.

Birte Pfleger: He's such an unlikely person to become such an important man in history. He was born out of wedlock in the West Indies. His mother had a really, really hard time with men: divorced, then a relationship with Hamilton's father, who she could not marry. Hamilton is an orphan by the time he's 14 years old, he struggled. That he survived is a miracle. Your chances of dying in late 18th century West Indies were higher than not dying, and he makes it out of there. He was very fortunate to have some people who became his supporters, his benefactors, and that's how he ended up in New York when he was nineteen and he started going to college.

Jim Keily: He started as a bastard child in the West Indies and got noticed when a hurricane hit the island and he wrote about it, his writing got noticed. Some of the folks said, "let's send him to the U.S. and get him educated" and by the time he's twenty, he's serving alongside General George Washington in the Revolutionary War. And he really became a great man, he was compelled to be great.

Birte Pfleger: He becomes involved in politics, he begins to write and he begins to write convincingly, compellingly. As a young man, he knew poverty, he had seen it, he had experienced it. And more importantly, he had experienced not having pedigree, not coming from wealth, not coming from a legitimate family, and that really shaped his life. It shaped him in that he always had a chip on his shoulder, he didn't want to be reminded of this childhood, and he also was a little arrogant.

Jim Keily: Hamilton was a man of the people in terms of his background and his story, but what he aspired to be was very different. He very quickly married into money, he very quickly decided that, in general, the masses lacked judgement, he didn't believe that there should be a massive voice given to the underclass as he thought they should do the heavy lifting and the elites should be in charge of policy.

Birte Pfleger: Alexander Hamilton's life does embody the American dream, which is, of course, a metaphor that did not exist in the 18th century. But he is everything that people think might happen to one who emigrates.

Jim Keily: He had a vision for America that was one of industrial power and military might. That was a huge contrast to some of the other Founding Fathers like Jefferson and Madison, who saw us as an agrarian society with a large middle class and just fringe elements on the upper and lower classes, and the fact that it was his vision that prevailed is what people will look at today that point to what some might consider the greatness of America, so I would suggest that his significance is the financial institutions and the economy that we have is all based on his principles, really his alone.

Birte Pfleger: Alexander Hamilton was a true capitalist, a true capitalist who believed that free trade was best for the country, was best for merchants and was best for customers. It would lower prices, it would produce better products. At the same time, he would not recognise the system we have today. He was certainly not a supporter of the government supporting ordinary people, but no one in the 18th century was.

Jim Keily: He thought that in order for us to become taken seriously in the world, we needed to ally ourselves with the great financial institutions in other countries that were well-off. He said to do this we must establish credit worthiness, and to do that, we must have debt. So he's suggesting to a country of people who have no money that what we need to do is take on debt in order to prosper, and so he took on all the state debts, consolidated them and sold them, sold all that debt off as bonds. And what that does, is it gives the elite, the people who have money, the ability to literally invest in the success of the nation. That in itself established us as creditworthy because we were paying back these bonds and the rest of the world started sitting up and taking notice.

Beginning with an opening song that summarises his childhood, Lin Manuel-Miranda's *Hamilton* traces the story of Alexander Hamilton's life, from being raised as an orphan in the Caribbean through to his

▲ *The Founding Fathers of The United States.*
Constitutional Convention, 1787.

death in 1804 at the hands of arch rival Aaron Burr. Over its two acts, the play touches on Hamilton's personal life, professional achievements, political ideas and his relationship to other renowned historical figures, with many critics commenting on its mature and nuanced depiction of America's Founding Fathers.

Michael Riedel: The examination of Hamilton's life in the show concentrates on his immigrant and outsider status. He could never be elected President because he wasn't born here in America. He was an outsider who could make it, because he was creating the establishment that he was going to make it in. He was inventing himself and the country at the same time. And that was an interesting insight that's in the book and that's in *Hamilton* the musical.

Anthony DeCurtis: Often when we are presented with the Founding Fathers, it's either in a very religious way, in which there's a kind of pantheon of saints, or it's the opposite: you tear this one down, that one had slaves, this one is problematic for this reason or that reason. And I think *Hamilton* really presented these characters in three dimensional terms and in recognisably contemporary terms, which is why I think a lot of young people like it.

Michael Riedel: It's important to understand with *Hamilton*, and the founding of this country, that you cannot think of the thirteen colonies as you think of America today. Georgia was not the same of Massachusetts. They had entirely different economies. For one thing, the South had slaves, slavery was a huge part of their economy, and, of course, the North had abolitionists; so they had to make an uneasy compromise over that. *Hamilton* does a good job of showing you that there were diametrically opposed interests at the founding of this country. And these men who forged the Constitution, who brought these colonies together, had a lot of very, very tough disagreements with each other, but still managed to persevere. It reminds us that this country almost didn't come together and there were no guarantees that they were going to succeed in creating the United States of America. But *Hamilton* shows that in the end, they rose above intractable disagreements, hatred for each other, to create a country.

Among the historical figures that appear in Hamilton are George Washington, Thomas Jefferson, James Madison, King George the Third and the Marquis de Lafayette. It is the lesser-known Aaron Burr, however, that takes centre stage as the former Vice President of the United States and key character in the *Hamilton* narrative.

Jason King: I think the dramatic core of *Hamilton* is the relationship of Hamilton to Aaron Burr. A contentious relationship. He went to Aaron Burr initially for mentorship, they had a lifelong relationship, and then Aaron Burr ended up killing him. That's really the centrepiece of the entire

▲   *Aaron Burr*

show, that powerful fraternity between the two that ends up in fratricide.

Birte Pfleger: Where to start with Aaron Burr? I think it's all about Aaron Burr's childhood. He lost his mother very early on, and I think that made Aaron Burr into an arrogant man, an insecure man, and also one who was looking for parental figures all his life and did not find them. He was also not as happily married as Alexander Hamilton was.

Aaron Burr and Alexander Hamilton met while they were both aides to George Washington. Both men were in their early twenties, and while they should have been getting along quite well because they had equally lonely teenage years, and politically they actually had similar views, both of them were federalists. But, nevertheless, they did not like each other personally because I think in some ways they were too similar.

Burr was also someone who was even more arrogant than Hamilton, and somehow they just did not get along.

Jim Keily: The bitterness between Aaron Burr and Alexander Hamilton goes back to 1791 when Hamilton's father-in-law, Philip Schuyler, was unseated in the Senate by Aaron Burr. His father-in-law would have supported the same kind of federalist policies that Hamilton endorsed and so he didn't really care for Aaron Burr for quite a long time. Then in 1800, when there was an Electoral College tie, Hamilton worked behind the scenes to see that the tie between Burr and Jefferson was broken with Jefferson becoming President, even though he couldn't stomach Jefferson, he liked him better than Burr.

Birte Pfleger: In the election of 1800, we have this really weird scenario where Thomas Jefferson, the anti-federalist or Democratic Republican at this point, is elected President. And Aaron Burr, who gets the second most votes but who was a federalist, becomes the Vice President. It's a scenario that we can no longer imagine - it's Clinton becoming president and Trump becoming vice president. So the Vice Presidency of Aaron Burr is already not something that that he really wanted, it's a very powerless position, even though one is a heartbeat away from the presidency, and Aaron Burr was trying to figure out how he could become president.

Jim Keily: Four years later, when it became apparent that Burr wasn't going to be the vice president again should Jefferson be re-elected, he chose to run for the governorship in New York, and that's where Hamilton campaigned heavily against him. Apparently a letter was written that got published in a newspaper suggesting he had made "despicable remarks". At that point, Burr sent Hamilton a letter to say, "what were

▲ *Alexander Hamilton & Aaron Burr prepare to duel. Weehawken, New Jersey, 1804.*

those remarks? I want you to acknowledge them or deny them" and Hamilton says, "I don't know. You have to be more specific" and they went round and round until eventually it resulted in Burr challenging Hamilton to a duel. Hamilton could have ended it by simply saying, "if I've said anything to offend you, it was unintentional". That would have done it. Hamilton did have an abhorrence for duelling, he suggested that it was completely uncivilised, he was against it, yet his pride was on the line.

Birte Pfleger: Alexander Hamilton despised Burr at this point for so many different reasons, and they keep writing about each other. They meet at this last event where Hamilton sings a song - that's in real life, not in the musical - and there were these insults, insults about women, insults about politics and Burr and Hamilton, because of these childhoods they had and because of their arrogance and because of their, at this point, already quite antiquated, notions of honour, decide they're going to have this duel. Hamilton writes a long list of the pros and cons, and then he proceeds. I think he knew he was going to die. I don't think Burr gave it as much thought as Hamilton did, I also think that Hamilton wanted to miss the shot. Burr did not.

Jim Keily: Hamilton expected, I believe, that they would probably shoot in the air, or actually the tradition at the time was when you fire your first shot, if your message is "I don't intend to fire at you", you shoot directly into the ground. Hamilton, by all accounts, may or may have fired accidentally, he shot into the air and it went into a tree behind Burr. Burr might have thought, "well, he didn't fire into the ground, he was aiming for me" and he turned around and shot Hamilton. It's also possible he wasn't trying to hit Hamilton, it's possible he likewise was intending to miss, but pistols back then oftentimes went far off from their targets. In the end, it's hard to say, they really don't know who actually took the first shot because there's a discrepancy in the telling.

Birte Pfleger: Hamilton then dies, and dies excruciatingly, twenty-six hours after the duel. He has a chance to say goodbye, and that's the end of a rivalry that began in the late 1770s and lasted a good twenty-five years.

As well as their deadly encounter on the banks of Hudson, the play depicts Burr's refusal to assist Hamilton in the drafting of the Federalist Papers, and introduces the audience to some of the central ideas in Hamilton's political philosophy.

Birte Pfleger: The Federalist Papers are a series of essays that Alexander Hamilton and James Madison wrote together to persuade Americans to ratify the Constitution, to understand the Constitution, to understand why there needed to be a separation of powers, why a republic was the only way a country could survive. Why we needed to have a House of Representatives that was popularly elected, but why we always also needed Senators who would, at that point at least, not be popularly elected and who would be in office longer than members of the House. Why we needed to have an independent judiciary, why we needed to have a limited executive, why we needed to have a Treasury, why we needed to have a Bill of Rights eventually.

This theme is further explored in the show through Hamilton's relationship with both Thomas Jefferson and James Madison, played by Daveed Diggs and Okieriete Onaodowan, which sets out the competing visions that the trio had for the future of the USA.

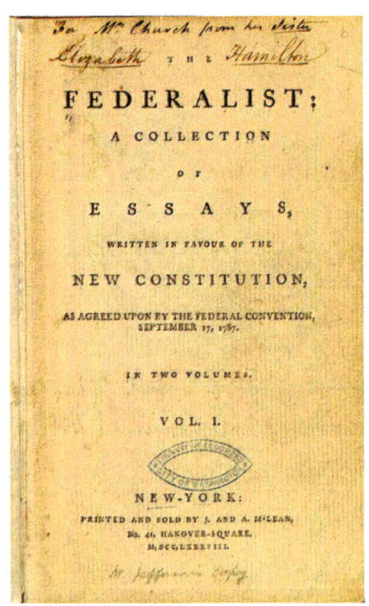

▲   *The Federalist Papers*

▲ *Thomas Jefferson*   ▲ *James Madison*

Jim Keily: Hamilton's relationship to Jefferson and Madison was one of contemporaries. They all started out as federalists, believed in a central government, but diverged in terms of how strong that central government should be, and so if there was personal animosity, it was grounded in their political ideologies and the differences between them more than actual bitterness, because they all started off together. They had decent working relationships where they drifted apart. The most, I think, was in Hamilton's insistence on a national bank and tying ourselves to big money interests, where Madison and Jefferson both sincerely believed that we should be an agrarian society and not be tied to European banks. An agrarian society, at least in the way that Jefferson and Madison saw the country, would have been mostly farmers and that our greatness would lie not in the extension of our economy to European economies, but more in westward expansion, and that in that westward expansion, we would find a nation of farmers who are self-sustaining and sustain themselves by selling our goods to the rest of the world as well, and that we would be reliant on a farming culture more than an industrial one.

Birte Pfleger: James Madison became Alexander Hamilton's enemy after 1790, after Washington is no longer president. Madison becomes an anti-federalist, he joins forces with Thomas Jefferson in the belief that a strong central government can turn on its people. Madison believed that the federal government needed to step back, and that we needed an agrarian society, and both Jefferson and Madison wrongly believed that it would take a thousand years to settle this country East to West. I think Hamilton understood somewhere, somehow, that it was going to be much faster than this and that the country needed to make preparations for growing, for increased commerce, for increased competition with other countries and for treaties with other countries.

Finally, the musical explores Alexander Hamilton's personal life, his marriage to the wealthy Elizabeth Schuyler in 1780, his extra-marital affair with Maria Reynolds and the tragic death of his eldest son Phillip, who is fatally wounded in a duel, in a grim foretelling of the fate that would later befall Alexander. It is Elizabeth Schuyler, however, who takes centre stage in the *Hamilton* narrative.

Birte Pfleger: He was really good looking, he was a great writer, a good talker and very charming, apparently. In 1779, he knew he needed to get married and he made a rather long list of things that he wanted in a wife. When he met Eliza Schuyler, she was all that and more, this amazing woman who couldn't have loved him any more, and I think it's very appropriate that the musical begins with her and it ends with her.

Despite the centrality of Alexander Hamilton's work to the founding of the nation, it's economic structures and, through the Federalist Papers, it's understanding of the Constitution, his legacy has remained obscure, eclipsed by the more glamourous characters of the period, like George Washington and Benjamin Franklin. For many Americans, Lin-Manuel Miranda's play would have been the first real encounter with the unrecognised face on the ten-dollar bill.

Jim Keily: Hamilton, before the musical, would have been remembered by historians and students of history, but not so much by popular culture, because it's kind of a dry telling, if you really think about it. He's about financial institutions and things that are complex, that most Americans don't want to actually think about because it makes their head hurt. So Hamilton was not a guy that you would speak about like you would with the other Founding Fathers, he wasn't Ben Franklin, he wasn't the great inventor, and he wasn't a President. He wasn't born in the U.S., he couldn't be a President, and he only lived to be forty-eight anyway, so as part of American culture, Hamilton was not a guy that you generally sit around talking about at the dinner table. And I think that's why Lin-Manuel correctly identified this as someone whose story is a little bit outside of the mainstream and worthy of telling, as opposed to the mythic figures that we're familiar with, like Jefferson and Washington and the first Presidents. Alexander Hamilton could certainly embody the great American immigrant dream, someone who came from nothing, came to the United States, and not only does well, he changes the course of history and defines what the entire country was going to be about. If there's ever a story of an immigrant that came here and achieved something great, I can't think of anyone who had a greater contribution than Alexander Hamilton. He is not just responsible for the money we spend, he's actually on it.

Birte Pfleger: Alexander Hamilton is very important to the modern world, especially in light of the 2008 worldwide economic crisis, the kind of avarice, what he would have called avarice. The financial turmoil that was created by these large financial institutions would have truly troubled Alexander Hamilton. This was not what he wanted to create. Yes, he wanted free markets, he wanted regulation, he wanted a central government that had a central bank, but he wanted that central bank to also keep control over the currency and to keep control over these businesses, to make sure that they could not basically run the world economy into the ground.

In its 'warts and all' depiction of Alexander Hamilton's life, the play presents a three-dimensional view of the Founding Fathers, one which isn't afraid to show them as flawed human beings. Hamilton biographer Ron Chernow described it as 'history for grown ups'.

Jim Keily: Approaching history in a way that doesn't deify the Founding Fathers, makes those characters all the more compelling. Historians don't always do that, they tend to mythologise Thomas Jefferson and suggest, for instance, that it was never in his character to have fathered children with a slave, and when you look at the evidence, it overwhelmingly supports the contrary - and I think those are the things that actually make those characters real, those are things that we identify with. When you deify somebody, they become as interesting as the statues that we erect to them, as opposed to the flaws that truly make someone human.

Leslie Odom Jr.: I think that's what's connecting people, just the humanity of it. I think people are seeing themselves in how flawed these people are, and it's giving them hope because of the wonderful things these people were still able to achieve, even with their flaws.

▲ *Aaron Burr kills Alexander Hamilton. Weehawken, New Jersey, 1804.*

Jim Keily: American history has had a long tendency to mythologise the Founding Fathers and those who came after. And there has in general been a whitewashing of American history, it's a history that's grounded in racism, our biggest problems stem from the institution of slavery and how we've treated minorities ever since. To say nothing of conquering a land that, according to American myth, was waiting for us, if you don't count the fact that there were already hundreds of thousands of people living here that needed to be removed in the white European estimation. Is there a tradition of whitewashing American history to make us feel better and, again, glorify our past? Well, absolutely. I think we're getting away from that more and more, but it's a long overdue process.

Michael Riedel: We tend to think of our Founding Fathers as these figures on Mount Rushmore, they're made of granite. Lin made them flesh and blood, he made them human. You saw the bickering, the squabbling, the dirty political compromises they had to make. You saw their burning ambition, you saw the hatred between Burr and Hamilton, the jealousy that Burr had for Hamilton's success, and that Hamilton outfoxed him at every turn. It reminded me very much of another great American musical called *1776*, which I know had a big influence on Lin, written by the great writer Peter Stone. And that show, before Lin got there, also made the Founding Fathers vital flesh and blood characters. There they have their faults, they can be petty, they can be envious. They also happen to be brilliant and were guided by a principle ultimately larger than themselves, and that was to create a country of diverse people.

Jesse Green: *Hamilton* certainly is history for grown-ups. I wouldn't say that's so radical. I think the idea of writing about and thinking about the failings of politicians is not new. There have been shows about politicians and they examine their inefficient love lives and other problems about them. I think what was more radically different about *Hamilton* is that it's a show about a politician that is also about policy. There is a tremendous amount of material in *Hamilton* about banking policy, about dealing with the French Revolution, about slave owning. It is not merely about Hamilton's biography. It is unique in musical theatre, as far as I know, with *one* exception, in dealing with the policy questions that animated the politicians we take an interest in. The exception was a show called *1776* about the ratification of the Declaration of Independence, which is a show that Lin-Manuel Miranda explicitly refers to in *Hamilton* and was obviously aware of as a forebear. How does it happen in *Hamilton* that you get ten more layers than you get in a *1776*? Or in a show like *Fiorello*, which is about an early mayor of New York, but is like a piece of dust compared to the depth of

Hamilton. And for that, you have to look at the construction of the songs.

But in taking such an approach to its subject, *Hamilton* inevitably opened a debate about historical accuracy, with some critics noting that the show side-steps some of the more uncomfortable questions of the time - in particular, the attitude of the main protagonists towards slavery.

Anthony DeCurtis: I think one of the most exciting things about *Hamilton* is the level of conversation about American history that it's provoked. People argue that Hamilton wasn't as against slavery as the play depicts. The Schuyler family that he married into, they were slaveholders. What was Hamilton's attitude about immigrants? People have contested that. There are all of these questions that have come up. I think most of the criticism of the play has been those kinds of debates: is this an accurate portrayal? Is it a fair portrayal? What corners is it cutting?

Jim Keily: You can say that of anything that's based on an historical event, that there should be a more balanced approach. But I don't think it's balance, so much as telling a story that has two sides of the same coin. In his instance, it's the contradiction of being a self-made man coming from nothing, and yet his vision for America's greatness lies in elites ruling. They go hand in hand, and to not examine one is to leave something out that I think is integral to his character and to his story. Nonetheless, what is there is accurate.

3. THE MIXTAPE

Inspired by Ron Chernow's thrilling narrative, which had previously been optioned no less than three times by Hollywood, Lin began to write new material around Hamilton's life, a life which had a natural dramatic arc of striving, success, sex, violence and tragedy. He called the project *The Hamilton Mixtape*.

Lin reached out to Chernow, inviting the historian to a performance of *In The Heights* and asking him to come on board the fledgling *Hamilton Mixtape* project as a historical consultant. In the early summer of 2009, he closed a programme of performances at The White House, "An Evening of Poetry, Music & The Spoken Word", with the opening number from the *Hamilton Mixtape*. Michelle Obama snapped her fingers in time as Lin rapped his story of "the Founding Father without a father". When he was done, Barack Obama led the White House audience in a standing ovation. The world had had its first, small glimpse of *Hamilton*, and a buzz started

▲　*The Cast of Hamilton at The White House, 2016*

amongst industry insiders that Lin-Manuel Miranda was working on something...intriguing.

Michael Riedel: The White House is a pretty good showcase for any little tune that you want to get out there, but I would say in the theater world the initial reaction to the idea was sceptical. I mean, a hip-hop musical about the Founding Fathers and, by the way, they're all going to be played by black people and Hispanic people and no white people. But there was a workshop, very private, for friends of Lin and the backers of the show, and I happened to have a few spies there. I heard that people were really impressed. They thought the songs were terrific, he's created these compelling characters around the Founding Fathers, it doesn't feel starchy, it doesn't feel historical, it feels contemporary, it feels vital, it has tremendous theatricality and energy. And that's when I began hearing, "you should keep your eye on this show. Just keep your ear to the ground, find out what's going on here", and after each subsequent workshop, you hear, "it's getting better, it's getting better" and then the money people started to hear about it and more people wanted to get into the workshops, and pretty soon they were writing checks to put the show on Broadway.

When he appeared at the White House, and we have to remember, Lin-Manuel Miranda was known to those of us in the theater back then, but not to the world at large, it was probably that rap that he did for the Obamas that set him on his way to becoming the celebrity that he is today, and I think the Obamas' endorsement of *Hamilton* has made it into the phenomenon that it is today.

The real standout from the White House show, however, was that the *Hamilton Mixtape* was, as its name suggested, all about hip-hop. When Lin-Manuel stood rapping in front of the President, it was clear

▲ *Lin-Manuel Miranda*

to observers that he was planning to try and succeed where others had previously failed, and write a play that had hip-hop as its main musical idiom.

Lin-Manuel Miranda: We're telling a story with music, on stage, so it's a musical. That's really the only definition of musical theater: telling a story on stage through music, punto. On everything else, it's up to you to write the rules. And for me, the fun was, you know, if that initial inspiration was that Hamilton is a singularly hip-hop character, you can't tell his story in any other musical genre. He uses more words than any of the other founders, he leaves behind more writing than any of the other founders; if you did an opera, it would be a day long. You need hip-hop because hip-hop has more words per measure than any other genre of music. And also, it has that energy, that energy of making something out of nothing, of writing so well about your circumstances that you transcend them.

Hamilton began to take shape over the course of 2010-2012 as Miranda assembled the core creative team that would help realise his vision.

Alex Lacamoire, a Cuban-American musician and composer who had accompanied Lin on piano during the performance at the White House, took on the role of Musical Director for the project. Lacamoire had previously served as Musical Director on *In The Heights*, for which he had been recognized with a Tony Award for Best Orchestrations and a Grammy Award for Best Musical Theater Album.

In June 2011, *Freestyle Love Supreme* took part in a benefit for the Ars Nova Theater in Manhatten, and Lin performed a second song from *Hamilton*, this time the iconic *My Shot*. The Ars Nova event marked the first time that Thomas Kail, director of *In The Heights*, had seen the work live, he committed to joining the project as Director and was keen that the team increase their efforts to make *Hamilton* happen.

In January 2012 Lin-Manuel Miranda gave a performance of a full twelve numbers from *Hamilton* at the Lincoln Center, for *American Songbook*, the Center's annual celebration of the art of songwriting. The intimate audience of four hundred and fifty guests included many heavyweights from the theater press, who began to get excited. Jeffrey Seller, producer of both *Rent* and *In The Heights*, formally offered to come on board as Producer; by that summer, he had optioned *Hamilton* for his company, *Adventureland*.

Michael Riedel: Lin is very skillful about parcelling out what he's doing. A lot of artists don't want you to see it until it's finished, Lin writes a song and he can't wait to take a video of himself and post on Facebook. He got the buzz rolling with that, and he's a canny operator, he knew the tastemakers were in the house and he knew he can entice them with some good songs and he knew that, in this era of media saturation, where there

▲ *Oskar Eustis*

are so many things to distract us, it's very important to begin to plant the idea of your show in people's minds long before it opens: "*Hamilton's* coming, *Hamilton*, the all-rap version of the Founding Fathers, Lin-Manuel Miranda did *In The Heights*, he won the Tony Awards, he just performed at the White House". He understands that in a world where there's so many distractions, so many things vying for your entertainment dollar, so many things to do in New York City alone, that you have to plant the idea of the show in people's minds before the show opens.

Lin eventually sent a tape of songs to Oskar Eustis, artistic director of New York's Public Theater, when Eustis heard the tape, he immediately made a deal with Jeffrey Seller to develop the show at The Public, and *Hamilton* had its first home.

Michael Riedel: Oskar is the head of The Public Theater and he is a firm believer in diversity of voices. Which is good and bad, I certainly believe you never know where the hits are going to come from, they can come from anybody, but sometimes his agenda is embracing diversity so much at the expense of

▲　*Joe Papp*

quality. Oskar is, I think, an admitted Marxist. He's a total left-winger and his theater has a political agenda which is on the left. Lin is a man of the left and the themes in *Hamilton* really are fundamentally of the left. That's what Oskar responded to. That's the kind of theater he wants, and Lin delivered the goods.

Jesse Green: The Public Theater was founded in 1954 by an amazing impresario named Joseph Papp, who in popular culture emerged as the David, facing the Goliath of municipal indifference and cultural waste, to develop a theater that would bring serious work, a great deal of Shakespeare, to the masses. At the beginning that meant taking the *Merchant of Venice* on a bus around the city and doing it in playgrounds, over time, it led to the development of much larger productions at "Shakespeare in the Park", which every summer does two huge productions for thousands of people.

Michael Riedel: Joe Papp was a man of the left, The Public Theater is very closely identified with the left-wing in this country, the kind of plays that they've always done have had a left-wing point of view. Joe Papp had been a communist, in fact, and had been blacklisted, but Joe was also a man of the working class, his parents were poor immigrant Jews from Eastern Europe, he grew up with no privileges, but as a young man he fell in love with Shakespeare. He believed that Shakespeare and theater should not just be for the rich, they should be available to the poor and the working classes of America, and that Shakespeare has something to say to everybody, no matter where you stand in the economic strata. He developed free Shakespeare in the park - over the great objection of politicians in New York City, by the way, who worried those poor people wouldn't know how to behave and would mess up genteel, beautiful Central Park. But Joe Papp won those battles and created free Shakespeare and believed that it should be available to all; that's why he called his theater The Public Theater, because it's for the public.

Over the years he produced some great, great plays and musicals, including *A Chorus Line*, which began at The Public Theater in the 1970s. Joe Papp really backed young people who had ideas for shows, and when Michael Bennett went to see Joe with the idea for *A Chorus Line*, similar to Lin-Manuel Miranda and Oskar Eustis, all Michael had was the tape of the dancers talking about *A Chorus Line*; but Joe liked Michael, and he said, "fine, here's some money, go to work. I don't know what it is, I don't know what it's called, there isn't even a score yet, but I like you and you seem to have a lot of ideas, that's what I want coming out of my theater". And Michael created *A Chorus Line*.

Lin sent the tape to Oskar. I'm sure Oskar liked some of the tunes, but Oskar hadn't seen the script yet. He didn't know what the show was going to look like, but he liked what he heard, and more importantly, he liked Lin-Manuel Miranda. He believed that Lin-Manuel Miranda was a genuine artist who was going

▲   *The Public Theater*

to create something that he wanted to be a part of, and that is fundamentally the job of the artistic director. It's what Joe Papp did brilliantly, and it's what Oskar does: they back the people who are going to create the shows that we're one day going to be talking about. That's their job, and that's what The Public Theater has done for years now. What I find ironic is that The Public Theater was founded on the principle that theater should be for everybody, if you don't have money, you still should still be able to come to the theater. I got news for you. *Hamilton* on Broadway - if you're not rich, you ain't getting in, that's the irony of the success of the show.

Having secured a venue at The Public, Lin-Manuel Miranda, Thomas Kail, Alex Lacamoire and a small group of actors travelled to Poughkeepsie, New York state, to take part in the *New York Stage & Film* series of developmental workshops that were held at Vassar College over the course of a week. During the workshops, Miranda and Kail encountered Leslie Odom Jr., who would eventually assume the role of Aaron Burr, the villainous counterpart to Miranda's Alexander Hamilton.

Kail appointed a Production Designer, David Korins, to work on the stripped-down, timber set, and Paul Tazewell, another trusted hand from *In The Heights*, came in on costumes, with a brief to imagine a modern version of eighteenth-century dress.

On February 17th, 2015, the curtain rose at The Public Theater and New York City got its first look at *Hamilton*: it absolutely brought the house down.

Jesse Green: People in the theater are very aware of all kinds of things going on, at any moment, that the population knows nothing about. Nobody knew anything about this. Nobody really knew anything about *Hamilton* except people who read the gossip sites or the chat boards until it actually happened, that was part of the amazement of it. Yes, insiders had heard that this was coming, from workshops and developmental processes that had gone on, but really very few people knew about it. For most of the world, even New Yorkers, even sophisticated theater-goers, it was as if it erupted full-blown out of nowhere.

Michael Riedel: It would have been a risk to open a show like *Hamilton* on Broadway right away. Had they just opened on Broadway, it would not have opened with fifty million dollars in advance ticket sales. People wouldn't have understood it, they wouldn't have known what it was. By opening in The Public Theater, you have a small space, you're pretty much guaranteed an audience because The Public has people who subscribe to the theater, so you've got a built-in audience for it, you also then have the mainstream press reviews. So there's no risk for the commercial producer of *Hamilton*, he spent a little money developing the show, he opens in The Public, if the critics hadn't liked it, it would never have gone to Broadway and he would have been out, I don't know, a few hundred thousand dollars instead of ten or twelve million.

Jesse Green: The Public Theater provides for these shows not only a nurturing environment, where they can see the show up on stage, make changes before they have to make a permanent statement about what a show could be, but it also provides a kind of imprimatur of seriousness that is an important endorsement for certain kinds of theater. You wouldn't expect to find a commercial revival of *Hello Dolly* coming out of The Public Theater. It's not only that The Public Theater provides a nurturing environment for new work, but it also tells its audience that this is the kind of work that they are likely to enjoy. There's a very clear quality, often of political interest, definitely serious, that people know is going to come out of The Public Theater, and to the extent that a show needs to build from a core audience toward a larger audience, it's often useful that a show be able to be branded that way.

Michael Riedel: What happens is that you open at The Public, you already have this buzz building about the show. You have the critics coming in, they rave about it, you only have two hundred and fifty seats to sell a night. Every VIP in this country, believe me, was trying to get into that show, which just amped the buzz even further. So you have this phenomenon created in this tiny little theater that's going to have to explode eventually, and the only way it can explode is to go to Broadway and explode there.

It's kind of a brilliant formula, if you have a good show: keep the ticket tight, keep the buzz hot, make them want it. They can't see it at The Public Theater. They can see it on Broadway for a thousand dollars.

During its run at The Public, *Hamilton* became the beneficiary of a one-and-half-million dollar grant from The Rockerfeller Foundation to support its student outreach programme. Honoring the spirit of Joe Papp and his theatre, the programme provided for twenty-thousand pupils at New York's public schools, in particular those from low-income homes, to attend matinees of *Hamilton* as part of their education.

After four months of celebrated shows at The Public Theater, it came time for *Hamilton* to spread its wings and depart for the bright lights and big audiences on Broadway which, in the summer of 2015, was ready for a shake-up.

4. ON BROADWAY

In the summer of 2015 *Hamilton* prepared to transfer from its off-Broadway run at The Public to The Richard Rodgers Theater on Broadway. Housing a one-thousand, four-hundred seat auditorium, the Richard Rodgers' distinguished history began in 1925, when it opened as "Chanin's 46th Street Theater", a name shortened simply to the "46th Street Theater" in 1931, before being renamed again in 1990 in honor of the famed Broadway composer Richard Rodgers, whose credits include *Oklahoma! The King and I, Carousel* and *The Sound of Music.*

The Theater's proud history includes playing host to some of *Hamilton's* progenitors, including *1776* and *In The Heights*, although in recent years a truly groundbreaking production had graced its stage only rarely, as Broadway had started to eschew distinctive or adventurous new work, and retreated into a form of safe, corporate theater.

Michael Riedel: Lin-Manuel Miranda is a superstar because of a Broadway show, and it's been a long time since Broadway has created a phenomenon like Lin-Manuel Miranda. If you go back into the history of Broadway and its heyday in the '30s, '40s and '50s, many stars came out of Broadway: Robert Preston, Yul Brynner, Mary Martin, Ethel Merman, Angela Lansbury. These people were household names. But Broadway went through a very, very difficult period in the late '60s and into the '70s where New York City was going bankrupt. Times Square was dangerous, there was no such thing as a *Lion King* or a family show on Broadway in 1975, trust me. And popular culture tastes

◄ *Hamilton at The Richard Rodgers Theater, W 46th St, Manhattan*

had changed. Broadway, which once had given us the hit parade of songs by Cole Porter and Irving Berlin and George Gershwin, suddenly, in the era of The Beatles and The Rolling Stones and The Supremes and Motown, seemed totally antiquated and out of it. It felt that way for a long, long time until, I would say, the last fifteen to twenty years, where Broadway slowly has come back to the forefront of American popular culture, no more so than now, with the success of *Hamilton* and Lin-Manuel Miranda.

As I detail in the book *Razzle Dazzle: The Battle for Broadway*, which takes you through this dark time in Broadway in the '60s and '70s, Broadway, like many other businesses in New York City at that time, could not leave New York. Our manufacturing businesses left New York, our garment district left New York, tourism was practically non-existent, police were handing out flyers in Times Square in the '70s saying "leave this neighbourhood by 6:00pm because it's not safe". Where's Broadway going to go? What, New Jersey? No. Broadway had to survive, and it survived. The only way it knew how to survive was to find young, creative people, the Lin-Manuel Mirandas of their day, who created shows that suddenly became attractions that people wanted to see.

If you go back forty years, the Lin-Manuel Miranda of the early '70s was a guy named Michael Bennett, a choreographer who had this dream of a show about the dancers in the chorus of a Broadway show - the "Gypsies", we call them, not the stars, but just the kids who go from show to show to show. And one night he got them all together and they drank a lot of cheap red wine and he tape-recorded their lives, and from that he fashioned a show called *A Chorus Line*, which was the *Hamilton* of its day. And when that opened on Broadway in Times Square, at the Shubert Theatre, suddenly this business that had been moribund had life in it again, and people from all over the world wanted to see *A Chorus Line*.

▲ *A Chorus Line*

After *A Chorus Line*, you had a show called *42nd Street* that became hugely popular, and then in the '80s (and we have the British to thank for this) Cameron Mackintosh and Andrew Lloyd Webber came along with this completely cockamamie idea for a musical about children's poems, about cats, that turned into the most successful show in the history of Broadway and made so much money for this industry and for New York City that it began to lift the fortunes of Broadway. And then when you start to have things like *Les Miserables* and *The Phantom of the Opera* and *Miss Saigon*, you have a Broadway that is no longer the backwater of the entertainment industry, but a business that is literally making billions of dollars on these shows that travel all over the world. The Walt Disney Company sees how successful *Cats* is and decides, "you know what? We've got some cartoon movies that might make nice stage musicals, so why don't we have a shot with *Beauty and the Beast* and *The Lion King*?" Once Disney decided to come to Broadway in the early 90s,

▲   *Broadway, 2014*

that is when the real transformation of Times Square and the theatre district began, but it would not have happened without the British who recolonised that little patch of New York City in the '80s with those successful shows.

Jesse Green: By the time *Hamilton* was being developed, American musical theatre was in an amorphous and, you might say, almost morbid state of uncertainty about what it could be. The Rodgers and Hammerstein revolution of the '40s and '50s was long since completed, the follow up revolution of the '60s and '70s of folks like Stephen Sondheim and the conceptual musical that Hal Prince and Kander and Ebb did a lot to develop, that too had basically run its course. The pop-opera influence from England, Andrew Lloyd Webber, had definitely run its course. There were lots of attempts to find new voices for the musical: you couldn't be too flat out serious, that was dreary;

you certainly couldn't be too cheerful and old fashioned because people would snore; you couldn't have phantoms with masks singing at the top of their lungs. There were just a lot of things you couldn't do anymore and yet not a clear idea of what you could do.

That doesn't mean there weren't terrific musicals that came about during that period and I'm sure that Lin-Manuel Miranda was quite aware of them and absorbing them, but they weren't necessarily huge successes. A lot of musicals that came out of downtown, for instance, were reflecting a new sincerity and a willingness to tackle dark, difficult subjects difficultly instead of cheerfully. I'm talking about musicals like *Caroline, or Change*, about an African-American woman who's a maid in a Jewish home in Louisiana; the book was written by Tony Kushner, the playwright of *Angels In America*. I'm talking a play like *Fun Home*, which is about a lesbian coming of age and learning that her father was secretly a gay man - this is not material that you would have dealt with seriously or cheerfully in the past, let alone with the incredible delicacy that was brought to it and to these other shows I mentioned. So this is the moment in which Lin-Manuel Miranda is developing *Hamilton*, a moment in which there's no sort of consensus about what musicals can be now, but a lot of consensus about what they can't be and with an understanding that new voices, new characters who have not been seen on stage, treated seriously, need to be part of the story.

Jason King: The shows of the time tended to be jukebox musicals, and by that I mean musicals that would take an existing song catalogue by a pop artist or band and then create an original dramatic narrative around that song catalogue. *Jersey Boys*, for instance, which celebrated the music of Frankie Valli and The Four Seasons, *Mamma Mia*, which celebrated the music of ABBA. The industry had become relatively risk averse, they

▲   *Rent*

wanted to ensure that audiences could fill those seats and one way to do it was to rely on established catalogues and pop music, it could be a little bit lazy.

Michael Riedel: I think Lin would say that the most profound influence on him was *Rent*, Jonathan Larson's musical. And, sad to say, Jonathan Larson died suddenly of an aneurysm just the day before the show opened off-Broadway.

Michael Riedel: *Rent* is very, very important in the last twenty years on Broadway, particularly, I think, in Lin-Manuel Miranda's career, because before that time, shows had begun to seem old fashioned, or they were just family shows. You had the Disney shows, you had *Beauty and the Beast,* or you had the holdovers from the British-era: *Cats* was still going on. But those shows began to feel a little old. You had no musicals that spoke to young people going through their struggles in the 90s, and that was what *Rent* was. It was poor, struggling artists living in New York City at a time when many of them were being killed by Aids, and it had a rock and roll score. So it suddenly felt contemporary and it brought young people to the theatre and it brought the generation that would become the Lin-Manuel Mirandas, who fell in love with musicals because of *Rent*. They may have appreciated and loved *Oklahoma!* and *The King and I*, but those are old fashioned shows. *Rent* showed them that you can write a contemporary show and it can work in the Broadway theatre.

Indeed in 2021 Lin-Manual made his feature film directorial debut with *Tick, Tick...Boom!* a biopic of *Rent* creator Jonathan Larson that starred Andrew Garfield in the lead role.

In July 2015, however, he pulled on his eighteenth-century costume, and took to the famous stage at The Richard Rodgers as *Hamilton* opened on Broadway.

5. CURTAIN UP

*H*amilton premiered on Broadway on July 13th, 2015, an event that was splashed across the front page of the New York times. The play swiftly became the hottest ticket in town, with the President himself, Barack Obama, flying in from Washington to secure a place in the audience for curtain-up on July 18th. The cultural phenomenon of the decade had arrived.

Jason King: I first heard about *Hamilton* reading a newspaper article in which I had heard that Lin-Manuel had performed an early number from *Hamilton* in front of President Obama and, you

▲ *President Obama attends Hamilton, 2015*

know, he raved about it, and so there was a real buzz about *Hamilton* for a long time. When it appeared off Broadway, you couldn't even get a ticket, it was extremely difficult and there was an incredible buzz. Great reviews, major, major word of mouth; it was really one of those shows that just becomes a cultural moment, it becomes the hottest ticket in New York, the hottest ticket on Broadway and it becomes the thing that you have to do if you live here or if you're visiting New York. And then I did see it on Broadway a few months after it opened and it was incredibly impressive, particularly the writing. I mean, it just jumped off of the stage.

Anthony DeCurtis: A publicist in New York was begging me to go see it, saying "it's really good, it's like hip-hop and American history". I'm like, "Broadway does hip-hop. No, thank you". I finally just to, candidly, humour this guy, said, "okay, I'd like tickets for tomorrow". And I was just *knocked out*! It was the last thing I expected. It was just so *live*.

Jason King: The reviews for *Hamilton* were off the hook, it was really one of the best reviewed shows I can imagine. There's been a few moments in in my lifetime in American theater where there have been shows that are not really just shows, but are cultural movements in a particular direction: *Angels in America*, the George C Wolfe and Tony Kushner show in the mid 1990s was one of those shows where it just changed the nature of American theater altogether, and I think *Hamilton* is also one of those incredibly galvanising moments in American theater, where it's critically acclaimed and it's also commercially successful. There's a real consensus of opinion about it. It's just loved by people, loved by critics.

Jesse Green: I thought it was great. I terrifically enjoyed it. I did not think it was something completely new in musical theater,

▲   *Lin-Manuel Miranda as Alexander Hamilton*

I understand what people were getting at when they said that, but it's not really true. It used new things to do what musical theater always does, that said, it did it very well. I also felt at the time, and with benefit of hindsight, having seen it since then, that it wasn't perfect. That's why you have an off-Broadway production of a show that everyone knows is going to Broadway. You might say, "why don't you just open it on Broadway right away, since that's your goal?" Well, because you want some time to look at it in front of an audience and make changes. And one of the things that Lin-Manuel Miranda was kind of brilliant about was taking the time to let the show play and find out how he could fix it, sharpen it. There was a great deal of improvement between off-Broadway and Broadway, most of it in invisible little ways, but things that I felt were a little bit unclear or off point in the off-Broadway production were gone or sharpened by the Broadway production.

Michael Riedel: It was sharper, a little more polished. And that is always not such a good thing because when you see something at The Public Theater that is new and fresh, there's a kind of energy and excitement and vitality to it that you lose a little bit when you move to Broadway and you add all the bells and whistles of a Broadway set and you've rehearsed it. What I found disappointing most of all, though, was the audience. It was a show that celebrates diversity with the Founding Fathers being Latino and African-American, all minorities. The audience was entirely white and rich. And I looked around, and there were young people in the audience, but they were clearly, given the fact that they wore extremely expensive clothes, trust-fund babies. And I thought, how ironic, that a show about Alexander Hamilton, an immigrant who came from nothing and made something of himself, is at the centre of a show that can only be seen by the 1%. Also, the audience was annoying because they clearly had listened to the cast recording over and over again, so they were rapping along. There's nothing more annoying than have somebody behind you singing along with this show, and Lin is a talented guy but, you know, not every lyric is brilliant. And I remember there was one moment where Leslie Odom Jr., who plays Aaron Burr comes on, and he says, "my name is Burr, sir" and this moronic woman behind me said, "my God, he rhymed 'Burr' with 'Sir'! Lin-Manuel Miranda is a genius!" Have you ever heard of Stephen Sondheim? Lady, please.

Jason King: I think *Hamilton* is really about the American dream. The American dream is a mythology, it's the idea that anybody can rise to the top and can become successful if you pull yourself up by your bootstraps, if you work hard, if you have a strong work ethic, if you make the right moves, if you do the right thing, you can achieve. I think it's more of a mythology than reality, but it's certainly part and parcel of the history of musical theater. A lot of great musicals have been sort of promulgating the American dream, and I think Lin-Manuel, through the two musicals that he has really been known for, which is *In The Heights* in 2008 and then *Hamilton* in 2015 - they're both shows about the American dream, about aspiration, about striving to get to the top, about the nature of the American character itself and in that sense I think the musicals are showcases for ideas about the American dream. And he has pressed hip-hop into service of these ideas about what it means to achieve in America.

I think what what Lin-Manuel is trying to do is to first of all show that elements of Alexander Hamilton's life, the fact that he grew up in the Caribbean and then came to the United States as an immigrant, the fact that he kind of willed himself into being a learned scholar and somebody who had risen the ranks politically, that story of being an underdog and then becoming a mainstream icon is a story that we've seen before in hip-hop, whether it's Jay-Z or whether it's Public Enemy or whoever else, that is part of the narrative of hip-hop itself. And then, of course, all of the beefs and fights that Alexander Hamilton got into over the course of his long career run parallel to beefs and fights in hip-hop, which are part of the nature of the form itself. And the use of words and language that is so essential to the development of the Constitution, to the Federalist Papers, there's a parallel there, you could say, with the use of wordplay and language in hip-hop. So, the musical is a kind of media commentary on language and how important that has been to the founding of the nation, but also how important hip-hop has been to the founding of the nation. It's all of those things at once.

Michael Riedel: What he has managed to do with *Hamilton*, and I think this is one of the reasons why it's much better than *In The*

▲ *Lin-Manuel & the cast of Hamilton*

Heights and has become the phenomenon that it is, is that the show has gone into the past to discuss our Founding Fathers and the beginning of this country of America, and it has captured the political dynamic in the country today. We are a country that's divided between the left and the right. And in *Hamilton*, you see the Founding Fathers are divided, they're at each other's throats over very profound and serious issues that could have split them apart, but somehow they managed, through compromise, to come together to forge a country. And that, I think, is a theme and a message that has appeal today in a country that seems to be coming apart.

Critical acclaim for *Hamilton* was unanimous. The original Broadway production won The Pulitzer Prize for Drama, the Grammy Award for Best Musical Theater Album and no fewer than eleven Tony Awards from a total of sixteen nominations.

Alex Lacamoire was recognized for his orchestrations, Andy Blankenbuehler for choreography, Paul Tazewell for costumes and Holly Binkley for lighting design. But it was the cast that really caught the eye of their industry, racking up seven Tony Award nominations between them, including for Best Actor, Best Actress and Best Featured Actor, and it was the cast that provoked some of the most excited write-ups in the arts press, a cast the likes of which had never before been seen in musical theatre.

6. THE PLAYERS

Hamilton proved to be the perfect platform for a new generation of actors to show their talent as Lin-Manuel Miranda consciously sought to assemble a multi-ethnic cast. With almost all of its parts played by actors of color, *Hamilton* presented a bold statement about diversity and the nature of contemporary America.

Anthony DeCurtis: I think the statement is, "this is our history, too. We're here, and we can play these roles and we can make it our story".

Jason King: The thing that's most unique about *Hamilton* is the fact that you have a multiracial cast, largely African-Americans and Latinos, playing historical figures who are white in a musical that uses hip-hop as its dominant language, where people are rhyming and singing at the same time. We've never seen that on Broadway before. Never, ever seen that. And I think that is just so good. The idea that a cast that's largely of color would be the vehicle to explore and explain American history, particularly at the level of the government of politicians and the story of the Founding Fathers themselves, that you could insert people of color directly into that narrative at the highest levels, I think that is something that really was transformative. It was incredibly powerful and it turned this musical into a real cultural moment.

Jayson Rodriguez: It's so far back, the beginning of this country, it gets microwaved where it's "white people founded the country", "black people were slaves", you know, Latinos aren't even a part of

▲ *Lin-Manuel & the cast of Hamilton*

it until much later, Asian people much later, and it's much more complex than that and this idea of mixing the looks and visually updating it, but also challenging the conventions of what you learned, I think that's important for young people. "What is he trying to say with these pieces? Let me look into this myself after the play", this is who Hamilton is, this is who Jefferson really is, this is what slavery was like at the time. Finding that out. You buy a ticket for a great time, but then you walk out of there, and even as expensive as the tickets are, it's nowhere near the value of what you're taking away.

Jesse Green: The ethnicity of the cast is an interesting duality when you're watching it on stage. After about a minute, it makes no difference. This is the man who is James Madison, this is the man who is Thomas Jefferson, you're not thinking "why is Thomas Jefferson black??!" The theater is amazing that way. And when the question of slavery arrives, you aren't really feeling an irony just because it happens to be a black actor playing a slave owner. That said, the fact that the cast is so diverse, a few white people, particularly playing King George, but also Asian-Americans, Latin Americans, black, all kinds of ethnic backgrounds, a non-textual component that is not only key to the theme of the show, which is the important contributions made by outsiders to the creation of this country and to change that is always needed, but also to the idea that we are now in a moment when an enormous body of talent that has been suppressed is now going to begin to be seen. That's part of the excitement that I think people felt: "who are these amazing performers? Why haven't we seen them before?", because there was nothing to see them in, "well, I want to see more of them!". So then more will get written and we will see more of them. That's part of the excitement that people feel. How could there be so many people with so much to offer and yet we haven't heard of them and they haven't been able to offer it before. And that is also the immigrant experience.

Lin-Manuel Miranda: I've gotten emails from L.A. executives who say, "you've totally made me rethink the casting of this project or that project because I saw what an incredibly talented, diverse group of faces can do to an audience". That's wonderful, I think it's a wonderful feeling to have that kind of impact. When something has that kind of success, it reverberates.

Michael Riedel: Broadway for a long time was called "The Great White Way". That became kind of a disparaging comment because the shows were, by and large, white, and the audiences certainly were white. But as young people become more interested in Broadway since the success of *Rent*, they're not all white kids now, and they're bringing new voices and new music to the form of the musical theater, which I think is good and healthy in the long run. *Hamilton* is a show that says "it doesn't matter what color you are or what your background is or what your ethnicity is", that musical theater is an art form that you can thrive in, that you should be attracted to, that you can work in. Not only do we have *Hamilton*, we have a great show like *The Color Purple*, which is an all African-American cast, and it's a superb show. Even in the old warhorses like *The Phantom of the Opera* - they cast an African-American phantom. So we are blending ethnicity and diversity in all of our Broadway shows, and that can only be to the betterment of the industry and the art form.

Jason King: There has been so much exclusion in the theater in which people of color have generally only been able to tell certain kinds of stories and to say certain things on Broadway. Their involvement has been very, very circumscribed and limited. So, to tell not just any story, but a founding story of the narrative of American life has a kind of meta relevance. It's a commentary itself on the role of people of color in this country.

Jim Keily: I think the significance of having this widely diverse cast is to highlight the huge contradiction of what reality was at that time, versus where we are 250 years later. It's just so wonderful to see this diversity and to whatever degree it's true or not, believe that we are trying to achieve a color-blind society while telling the story of one that certainly wasn't.

I do believe that the ethnic diversity that is contained in the musical *Hamilton* does attach a sense of relevance to the story and makes history more accessible to its audience. Too often, even my own students come into college history class fully

▲ *Daveed Diggs, Leslie Odom Jr., and Renée Elise Goldsberry at the Tony Awards, 2016*

expecting to hate it. And whenever you can try and make it relevant and draw it to the here and now, they suddenly realise, it's not a static examination of a dusty old past, it's a continuous line that connects to the present. And I think this play, this musical, does achieve that brilliantly.

A host of standout performances earned the play's cast accolades and nominations, with Lin-Manuel Miranda as Hamilton, Leslie Odom Jr. as Aaron Burr, Philippa Soo as Eliza Schuyler Hamilton, Daveed Diggs as both Thomas Jefferson and Marquis de Lafayette, Johnathan Groff as King George III, Christopher Jackson as George Washington and Renée Elise Goldsberry as Angelica Schuyler all recognized for their work.

Leslie Odom Jr.: This show has helped me find some direction, helped me find some purpose again. This is what I always felt like I was meant to be doing, but I was waiting for Lin to write it.

Daveed Diggs: Getting to play a role where I get to take these things that I learned from just trying to walk around like my dad walks around, you know, has been so great. And Thomas Jefferson? Like, come on, there's no way that that should be real. That I should get to read lines written for Thomas Jefferson. It's been so great and it's been so much fun. One of the great things about this process is how much of ourselves we were asked to bring to it and how much sense it kept making to do that.

Anthony DeCurtis: I thought Lin-Manuel Miranda was great in his role as Hamilton. In a sense he was telling his own story, I feel like he very much identified with the character that he created. And Daveed Diggs, who played both Lafayette and Jefferson, moving between those two roles was really fun and exciting and intriguing to watch.

Michael Riedel: I think the real star of the show in terms of the acting was Leslie Odom Jr., who played Aaron Burr. I've been an admirer of his for a long, long time, he is a terrific actor. And Lin is certainly a talented guy, he created this show, but he was the weakest performer of them all because he's not a great actor. Leslie Odom was so charismatic and so compelling as Aaron Burr. It's always better, I think, to play the villain. It's just a juicier part, and Leslie played it with a kind of ferocity and an intensity that was pretty thrilling when you saw it, especially at the Public Theater, he was at this high level and Lin was still, you know, wobbling around down here trying to find the character. He was also writing the show and fixing the show, so he had a few distractions there, but Leslie, to me, was the real star of that show. And then Daveed Diggs, who played Lafayette and

Thomas Jefferson, became a favourite with everybody. I would say he was better when I saw it in The Public Theater, by the end of his run on Broadway, he'd become a little too plummy, a little too ripe in the role. Even his hair seemed to get bigger at the end of his run, he seemed to be enjoying a little too much the fame that was accruing his way. But that often happens, I mean, when you're in a phenomenon like *Hamilton* and suddenly you go from being, you know, no one knows who you are to being on the A-list at everybody's party in New York City, it's bound to make your hair grow a little larger.

Jesse Green: To me, it was the combination of all of them that was stunning. That they were able to find so many people who could perform that very difficult work so brilliantly, and now, with a second cast and with the touring cast, it's not like they're having a lot of trouble finding these people. They've been waiting for something to come along with which they could show who they are. Yes, I loved Renée Elise Goldsberry or Daveed Diggs or a different person, depending on what I'm listening to, but it was more all of them together that did it for me.

CAST PROFILES

Leslie Odom Jr. – Aaron Burr

Leslie Odom Jr. was born on August the 6th, 1981, in Queens, New York, and grew up in Philadelphia, Pennsylvania. He was educated at the Philadelphia High School for Creative and Performing Arts and honed his singing ability in his local church choir, where he was as soloist. Over the course of his career to date, he has developed a reputation as one of the most versatile performers of his generation.

Leslie's Broadway debut came at the age of seventeen when he appeared in *Rent*, and he has since built a diverse career in theater, television, film, and music. He became involved in *Hamilton* during the 2014 workshop at Vassar College in Poughkeepsie. Leslie was at the college to accompany his wife, who was taking part in a different reading. Initially skeptical about the project, he joined the workshop cast after seeing the material's depth and creativity.

Other notable roles that Leslie Odom Jr. has assumed include in the TV series *Smash* and the films *Harriet* (2019), where he portrayed abolitionist William Still, and *One Night in Miami* (2020), where he earned critical acclaim for his portrayal of the soul singer Sam Cooke. He has also pursued a successful music career, releasing several records including a self-titled jazz album and *The Christmas Album* (2020).

He won a Tony Award for Best Actor in a Musical for his performance in *Hamilton,* and was nominated for both an Academy Award and a Golden Globe Nomination for *One Night in Miami.*

Leslie is married to the actress Nicolette Robinson, together they have a daughter, Lucille Ruby, and a son, Able Phineas; he frequently credits his family as a source of inspiration and grounding in his life and career.

Daveed Diggs – Thomas Jefferson/Marquis de Lafayette

Daveed Diggs was born on January 24th, 1982, in Oakland, California. The son of a Jewish mother and African-American father he grew-up in a multi-faith, multi-ethnic household. He attended Berkeley High School in California and later pursued higher education at Brown University, where he earned a degree in theater arts. During college, he excelled as a track athlete, setting a school record in the 110-meter hurdles.

Daveed Diggs is an accomplished actor, rapper, writer, and producer. After an early career in experimental theatre, he collaborated with Lin-Manuel Miranda and Thomas Kail in *Freestyle Love Supreme*, where his rapping ability marked him out.

Miranda invited Diggs to participate in the early workshops of *Hamilton*, his unique energy, quick wit, and impressive lyrical skills made him a natural fit for the dual roles of Lafayette and Jefferson and his rapid-fire delivery and charismatic performances garnered widespread acclaim, helping to catapult him to international fame and a multifaceted career in entertainment.

In addition to his work in theater, Diggs is a co-founder of the experimental hip-hop group *Clipping.*, which combines narrative-driven lyrics with innovative soundscapes. He has starred in numerous films and television series, including *Blindspotting* (2018), which he co-wrote and starred in, and shows like *Snowpiercer* and *Black-ish*. Diggs has also lent his voice to animated projects, including *Soul* (2020) and *The Little Mermaid* (2023).

Daveed Diggs is in a long-term relationship with actress and writer Emmy Raver-Lampman, who performed as part of the ensemble in *Hamilton*, where she was also understudy for all three main female roles. Daveed often speaks about his deep connection to his hometown of Oakland and how its cultural diversity has shaped his artistic vision. His dual performance as Jefferson/Lafayette earned him the Tony Award for Best Featured Actor in a Musical.

Phillipa Soo – Eliza Schuyler Hamilton

Phillipa Soo was born on May the 31st, 1990, in Libertyville, Illinois. Soo was raised in a supportive and artistic household. Her father, a doctor, is of Chinese descent, and her mother, of European descent, worked in the arts. Encouraged by her family to pursue her artistic interests, Soo developed a love for acting and singing early on. She attended Libertyville High School and later earned a Bachelor of Fine Arts degree in Musical Theater from The Juilliard School in New York City, graduating in 2012.

Phillipa made her mark as an actress and singer in musical theater. Shortly after graduating from Juilliard, she earned critical acclaim for her role in the off-Broadway production *Natasha, Pierre & The Great Comet of 1812*, where she came to the attention of Lin-Manuel Miranda. Impressed by her vocal range and emotional depth, Miranda invited her to join the workshop production of *Hamilton*. Her portrayal of Eliza, Alexander Hamilton's wife, brought nuance and heart to the story, earning her a Tony nomination for Best Actress in a Musical, and solidifying her reputation as a rising star in theater.

Since *Hamilton*, Phillipa Soo has appeared in other Broadway productions including *Amélie* (2017), where she played the title role, and *Camelot* (2023). She has also taken on roles in television and film, including voice work in the animated film *Over the Moon* (2020).

Phillipa Soo married actor Steven Pasquale in 2017. The couple is actively involved in the arts community and Phillipa is also passionate about philanthropy, she has participated in various initiatives supporting education and diversity in theater.

Renée Elise Goldsberry – Angelica Schuyler

Renée Elise Goldsberry was born on January the 2nd, 1971, in San Jose, California and was raised in Houston, Texas, and Detroit, Michigan, where her mother worked in the automotive industry, and her father worked as a chemist and physicist. Goldsberry showed a strong interest in the arts from a young age, especially singing and acting. She earned a Bachelor of Fine Arts degree in theater from Carnegie Mellon University and later completed a Master of Music in Jazz Studies at the University of Southern California's Thornton School of Music.

Renée Elise Goldsberry is an accomplished actress and singer with a career spanning theater, television, film, and music. Her Broadway debut came performing the role of Nala in *The Lion King*, followed by notable performances in *Rent* and *The Color Purple*. In television, she has appeared in *Ally McBeal*, *The Good Wife*, *Altered Carbon*, and *Girls5eva*. Her film credits include *Waves* (2019) and *The House with a Clock in Its Walls* (2018). Renée has also performed in concerts and released music.

Renée joined the cast of *Hamilton* after being introduced to Lin-Manuel Miranda's work through mutual connections in the theater community. She was cast as Angelica Schuyler in the Off-Broadway production and stayed with the show as it transitioned to Broadway, her portrayal of the fiercely intelligent and emotionally complex Angelica, including her performance of the show-stopping song *Satisfied* earned her widespread acclaim as well as the Tony Award for Best Featured Actress in a Musical, a Drama Desk Award for Outstanding Featured Actress in a Musical and a Lucille Lortel Award for Outstanding Featured Actress.

Renée Elise Goldsberry is married to attorney Alexis Johnson, with whom she has a son and an adopted daughter from Africa. She is deeply committed to balancing her professional and family life and is a strong advocate for adoption, and for representation in the arts.

Christopher Jackson – George Washington

Christopher Jackson was born on September the 30th, 1975, in Cairo, Illinois.

Jackson grew up in a small-town environment, after discovering his passion for performing he attended the American Musical and Dramatic Academy (AMDA) in New York City, where he honed his skills in acting and singing, setting the stage for a successful career in theater and entertainment.

Christopher is an accomplished actor, singer, songwriter, and composer; he made his Broadway debut in 1997, playing Simba in *The Lion King*. From there went on to appear in numerous Broadway productions, including *In The Heights*, where he originated the role of Benny. Beyond theater, Jackson has worked extensively in television, with roles in shows like *Bull* and appearances in *The Good Wife*. He has also provided vocals for several animated projects, including for the character of Chief Tui in Disney's *Moana* (2016), and contributed to the world of music as a songwriter and performer, collaborating with artists like Will Smith and LL Cool J.

Christopher Jackson's involvement in *Hamilton* stemmed from his long-standing collaboration with Lin-Manuel Miranda. After his work on *In The Heights*, Miranda invited Jackson to participate in *Hamilton* from its earliest developmental stages. His portrayal of George Washington—imbued with authority, grace, and humanity—became one of the standout performances of the musical and brought him a Tony nomination for Best Featured Actor in a Musical, an award that was ultimately given to his co-performer, Daveed Diggs.

Jackson is married to Veronica Vazquez, a theater performer and producer. The couple have two children, one of whom is on the autism spectrum. Jackson is an outspoken advocate for autism awareness and dedicates time to promoting understanding and support for the autism community.

Jonathan Groff – King George III

Jonathan Groff was born on March the 26th, 1985, in Lancaster, Pennsylvania.

Groff grew up in a Mennonite religious community in the rural town of Ronks, Pennsylvania with his mother, a physical education teacher, and father, a harness horse trainer; both his parents encouraged his artistic pursuits. The young Groff attended Conestoga Valley High School, where he developed a passion for theater and performing. After graduating in 2003, he deferred his acceptance to Carnegie Mellon University to join the national tour of *The Sound of Music*, which marked the beginning of his professional acting career.

As an actor and singer, Jonathan Groff has a celebrated career, with work that spans theater, film, and television. He made his Broadway debut in *In My Life* (2005) but rose to prominence with his Tony-nominated performance as Melchior Gabor in the original Broadway production of *Spring Awakening* (2006).

On the small screen, Groff gained recognition for his roles in *Glee* as Jesse St. James and in the Netflix crime drama *Mindhunter* as FBI agent Holden Ford. On the big screen he is known as the voice of Kristoff in Disney's blockbuster *Frozen* franchise.

Groff joined *Hamilton* in 2015, taking over the role of King George III from Brian d'Arcy James during the off-Broadway run at The Public. His comedic timing, charismatic stage presence, and distinctive rendition of King George's songs quickly made him a fan favorite.

Though his role in the musical was relatively small, Groff's performance added a unique flavor to the show, consolidating his reputation as one of Broadway's most versatile performers. His performance of *You'll Be Back* became iconic, earning him widespread acclaim and a Tony nomination for Best Featured Actor in a Musical.

Groff is openly gay and an advocate for LGBTQ+ rights. He publicly came out in 2009 and has been candid about his journey. He values privacy in his personal life but has spoken about how his upbringing and experiences have influenced his artistic choices.

7. THE MUSIC

As with any work of musical theater, the real star of the show is the music itself. Although Lin-Manuel's starting intention had been to develop *Hamilton* as a hip-hop musical, in train with his description of the historical Alexander Hamilton as a "singularly hip-hop figure", it was an ambition that was fraught with risk. While previous attempts to integrate hip-hop and musical theater had been unsatisfying, with *Hamilton* Lin was undertaking the task of trying to succeed where others had failed: to make hip-hop a success on Broadway.

Jayson Rodriguez: Hip-hop and theater have kind of had a slowly developing relationship. Hip-hop is this dominant force in pop culture and there have been attempts at blending hip-hop

▲   *The cast of Hamilton perform musical selections from Hamilton at The White House*

and theater in the past, whether it was Mos Def being in *Topdog/ Underdog*, Savion Glover with *Bring In 'Da Noise, Bring In 'Da Funk*, Puff Daddy had a major role in *A Raisin In The Sun*. Then here comes *Hamilton* and it's this big, towering success, but it comes from a road that was paved by other people - you can argue that hip-hop has had trouble on Broadway and in theater productions, or you can just say it's had its incremental success.

Jason King: There have been many attempts historically to try to incorporate hip-hop into musical theater. In particular I'm thinking of *Bring In 'Da Noise, Bring In 'Da Funk*, the George C Wolfe directed show that starred Savion Glover, that was a mix of rap and funk and hip-hop, and that was quite successful in its time. But I think, generally speaking, hip-hop as a form pursues a certain kind of authenticity that is very much related to street credibility, that is very much rooted in the blues, where you live the life that you sing about in your song or that you rap about in your song. There's a way in which that rubs up against the kind of expressive inauthenticity of musical theater, which is often very campy or over the top. I think there's an impasse there, where the grittiness and the urban aspects of hip-hop just don't really seem to fit on the musical theater stage.

Jayson Rodriguez: The main thing with hip-hop is this idea of authenticity. And it doesn't necessarily mean "you came from the hood and I came from the suburbs". I think a lot of authenticity is talent, right? Like, "are you talented?". Lin-Manuel Miranda has this elasticity to his rhymes that's very current and that's appealing to this massive audience, that went and saw the show, that was not a traditional Broadway audience. *Holla If Ya Hear Me*, the Tupac play, was on Broadway - great intentions, and the execution just seemed so over the top, it just felt a little bit corny, just not cool. With Lin-Manuel Miranda, what he was able to

▲   *Lin-Manuel Miranda*

do with *Hamilton* was cool. From the flow, to the cadence, to the way they were dropping on the beat, so much so that the soundtrack to *Hamilton* charted.

Jesse Green: What I do think is the core of the success of the use of hip-hop in *Hamilton* and what Lin-Manuel Miranda brilliantly has exploited, is the fact that in any one minute passage of a song in hip-hop, you will have four to ten times more words than you would in a traditional song, so he has the ability to provide four to ten times more information in any moment of the show. It's part of why the show is so overwhelming, you really are being given a ton of information at all times and it doesn't ever let up. So you're getting musical information, you're getting a tremendous amount of verbal information, and all the visual and emotional information that's coming at you, too. That's where the hip-hop really makes a difference, he could not possibly have told of the ambition of Hamilton, the love life of Hamilton, the failures of Hamilton, the duels of Hamilton, the policies of Hamilton, the feuds of Hamilton, all of these layers of the story in a traditional musical theater songwriting format. There's not enough space.

Lin-Manuel Miranda: Once I decided Hamilton is a singularly hip-hop figure, and this is all my first time reading the book, mind you, I go, okay, so what does he sound like? And that's how you start to build a score. All right, so he's going to be like my heroes - he's going to rhyme six syllables on a line if he needs to, he's going to be the son of Rakim, the son of Eminem, the son of big Big Pun, who has one of my favourite hip-hop lyrics of all time: "dead in the middle of Little Italy/little did we know that we riddled two middlemen who didn't do diddly". Lyricists that make you rewind them instantly because you can't believe how many rhymes have happened on the line. Those are the ones I love and the ones I keep coming back to, and Big Pun was a big one of those for me.

It took me a year to write *My Shot*, because *My Shot* is mostly in Hamilton's voice, and I wanted it to have those Big Pun-ish lines where every syllable is filled and making up at least a four syllable rhyme every time. So it's: "I'm a diamond in the rough", which is a Big Pun lyric, "a shiny piece of coal/trying to reach my goal/the power of speech is unimpeachable/I'm only nineteen but my mind is older", which is a Mobb Deep lyric, "these New York City streets get colder, I shoulder/every burden, every disadvantage/I have learned to manage, I don't have a gun to brandish/I walk the streets famished/the plan is to fan this spark into a flame/but damn, it's getting dark, so let me spell out my name". Even the end of line agrees with the beginning of the next line, so they have to follow each other and as strung together as like the best thick rope. So now what does everyone else sound like? Okay, so I'm reading through and reading about George Washington and I'm reading about him fleeing New York, and it's this moral authority, he's the only veteran we have. So it's very regimented, it's as regimented as military thinking is: "can I be real a second/for just a millisecond/to let down my guard and tell these people…" - there's no syncopation in it at all. It's super tak-tak-tak-tak-tak, because he's a military man, he likes a military rhyme. Thomas Jefferson - Thomas Jefferson misses most of the war, but he writes our founding documents, he writes the Declaration of Independence. But he's just been chilling in France, so I sort of cast him as the jazz that leads to hip-hop. So I listened to a lot of Lambert, Hendricks and Ross. I listened to a lot of Gil Scott-Heron. I listen to sort of the jazz that if you put a beat under it, it would be hip-hop, but it's jazz.

Jayson Rodriguez: You can trace influences like Slick Rick or Outkast, elements of Mobb Deep in the battle scene and those aren't easy things to balance and pull-off, it makes this unique pastiche. But what really makes it so incredible is the flow and the delivery. If somebody has a bad flow, you just don't care what they're saying.

Although the core of the music may have been hip-hop, *Hamilton's* score moves beyond a single genre, and incorporates a series of other styles, from beat music of the 1960s to traditional show tunes, in a sprawling, brilliantly creative melange of styles and influences.

Renée Elise Goldsberry: One thing that's beautiful about Lin-Manuel Miranda is that he really reflects the way we listen to music now. We listen to every kind of music, so every kind of music is useful when you're writing musical theater now. In this season alone, there's country music, there's hip-hop, there's classical, it's all there, it's all relevant, it all matters. And the most important thing as a performer that you can do is really have the confidence to know that what your voice is doing is right.

Jason King: The music of *Hamilton* is really interesting because although it is clearly rooted in hip-hop and some of the standout numbers in the show are the rap numbers, there's also a lot of other types of music in the show. There's kind of British pop music of the '60s, Monkeys, Beatles style music; there is R&B, there is more traditional Andrew Lloyd Webber style music in it. It's very, very diverse, much more than I think it's been given credit for; but of course, it's the hip-hop that's the lifeblood of the show. I think the introductory number, *Alexander Hamilton* is probably the most striking number in the show because it introduces you to the larger themes, the major characters. Lin-Manuel has this thing where the opening numbers for his shows, like in *In The Heights*, provide the narrative impetus for the entire show. They introduce us to all the themes, but they do it with this incredible wordplay, I remember seeing it on Broadway and just thinking, "wow!". People gave a standing ovation at the end of the opening number, it was that galvanising and that powerful.

Anthony DeCurtis: The depiction of King George III in the play is just hilarious because it works on so many levels. The music is very Beatle-esque which is a kind of a pun on the English and it's also a kind of pun on boomer culture and this young insurgent culture, because there's a very passive aggressive quality to Jonathan Groff in the original production and in his performance as King George III, he's dressed up like Elton John.

Michael Riedel: There are some beautiful, more traditional kind of musical theater numbers. Very melodic, Lin has a gift for melody, which I didn't appreciate the first time around. You can't have musical theater songs without a melodic line and sometimes with hip-hop and rap the melodic line is not that strong. So if you had a score that was just one hip-hop number at the after the other, I don't think it would be as successful as it is. He's found a way to vary it up, so I think a song like *The Room Where It Happens* is very, very powerful, it's a slowly emerging song of ambition and jealousy, of Aaron Burr saying, "why am I left out? Why am I not the one making the decisions? Why am I not there when this big stuff is going down?" So it's a very good character number, because it really shows you why Aaron Burr comes to hate Alexander Hamilton; a powerful, powerful number in the show.

Atlantic records released *Hamilton (The Original Broadway Cast Recording)* as an album in September 2015. It proved to be an enormous hit, becoming highest-charting cast album since 1963, peaking at number one on the Rap Albums Chart, the first cast album to ever do so, and number three on the Billboard Chart. The record won the Grammy award for Best Musical Theater album in 2016 and in 2023, *Hamilton* achieved diamond certification to become the best-selling cast album of all time.

Lin's score had managed to transcend the traditional frame of music-for-stage to become a successful, standalone work of popular music and with it, Miranda definitively proved that hip-hop could be a success on Broadway.

8. THE STAGING

In bringing *Hamilton* to life on-stage, Lin Manuel-Miranda turned to his firm friend and frequent collaborator, Thomas Kail.

Kail and Miranda first met while both were students at Wesleyan in the late 90s, where together they founded the hip-hop troupe *Freestyle Love Supreme*. In the years following graduation, Kail managed to gain directing experience with two on-Broadway plays: Julia Jordan's *A Bus Stop Play* (2007), and Beau Willimon's *Zusammenbruch* (2008). His breakthrough came, of course, with the musical that he had been developing with Lin, *In The Heights*, for which he was recognized with the Tony for Best Direction of a Musical.

▲ *Andy Blankenbuehler, Lin-Manuel Miranda, Alex Lacamoire & Thomas Kail*

After Lin had his original concept for *Hamilton*, it wasn't long before Tommy joined the project as director, bringing focus and drive to the development phase and playing a crucial role in putting together the production team, conducting many of the interviews himself.

One of Kail's key early appointments was David Korins as Production Designer. Korins's concept was to have the stage appear as if it were mid-construction, to reflect the theme of American being built by the Founding Fathers as a work-in-progress.

Together with Korins, Andy Blankenbuehler on choreography, Paul Tazewell on costumes, Howell Binkley on lighting and Nevin Steinberg on sound made up a core team notable for its pedigree and attention to detail. Tazewell had won acclaim for his previous work on *Bring in 'Da Noise, Bring in 'Da Funk* (1996) and *The Color Purple* (2006) and had been Tony-nominated for his previous work with Lin and Tommy on *In The Heights*. In imagining costumes for *Hamilton*, he looked back at the work of fashion designers who had themselves been inspired by the eighteenth century: Alexander McQueen, John Galliano and Jean-Paul Gaultier. Howell Binkley was a veteran of theater lighting, making his Broadway debut in 1993 with *Kiss of the Spiderwoman*, for which he was nominated for a Tony, an award he eventually won in 2005 for his work on *Jersey Boys*; as with the other guys, Howell had been a core part of the team on *In The Heights*.

With the band back together again, the staging of *Hamilton* came together in tandem with Lin's writing. Rather than wait for their guiding creative to finish his play in its entirety, the team worked around Lin to develop the show as he continued to draft and imagine it.

Thomas Kail: Lin wrote the first song in 2009, and it's June of 2016, so that's seven years of your life that you spend trying to take this little seed and grow it into not just a tree, but a forest. That's really what my job is, to try to create an environment where the writer can feel nurtured and supported and alive. And then I try to add other seeds around him and find other people to make me better and to try to realise the show.

Jesse Green: Thomas Kail did a lot of really smart things. Despite presumably knowing that he had an amazing property on his hands, he didn't overdo it. The staging is very stepped back when it needs to be, he gives space to the verbal component, which is a joy for theatergoers who remember when plays still were about words. It's been a long time since we've seen that to this degree, but then when the show needs to be paced and illustrated, he comes forward and gives us exactly what we need and not a lot more. So, for instance, in the staging of the duels, they're on a turntable, there's three of them, the bullet is sent flying from the gun of Burr in the form of an ensemble member who represents the bullet moving slowly across space. This has the effect not only of reminding you what's at stake, it's getting closer, but also slowing down the action just at the moment when you need to understand how important what's about to happen is, how it's going to change the fate of our country. So I think he really calibrated perfectly when to show off a little bit and when to pull way back and let the words show off.

Michael Riedel: His direction never got in the way of Lin's score and Lin's script. He's not a director who puts his thumbprints over everything. He understood that the power of the show was in the music, the lyrics and the storytelling and his direction is very skilful. You don't walk away from that show thinking, "Wow, who is that director? What an amazing production". You walk away from that show thinking, "My God, Lin-Manuel Miranda is a genius" and Tom understood that his job was to serve Lin's show.

Thomas Kail: The reality is, obviously everybody on stage and off stage in this company is working at the absolute top of their game. The baseline of everything is trust and faith, so that's why saying "no" isn't that hard. That's why saying "maybe" is also not that hard and saying "yes" isn't that hard. The reality is sometimes the best answer you can give is "keep going". It is very rare that I would ever do anything that would stunt or prevent anyone from taking an idea and fully expanding it, my job is to create a room where everybody knows what they're being asked to do, that everybody knows what story we're telling and how we want to tell it. Lin and I got to a place, and Alex and Andy share this, where it was almost subliminal. There were times when he would just cock his head and like, "I know, I know just let me go through the thing". But the reality is it was such a safe room for all of us that these actors also knew that they were allowed to live in a place where they could explore. And we tried to create that for each other.

Jesse Green: The physical production of *Hamilton* is quite interesting because each element draws from a different world. In a way the settings are very recessive, they pull back visually. There's not a great deal of visual information, which is a very wise choice. I think it is so important to hear the words and to focus on the words and to understand that that's where the information's mostly coming from. To have had a lot of visual information coming at the same time would have been catastrophic. So the design suggests a ship with wooden planks and some ropes and things like that, possibly the ship of state, but other than that it withdraws itself. To the forefront are the performances.

The lights, on the other hand, are very colorful and fast moving and always changing, much in the manner of arena rock and possibly a reference to the hip-hop aspect of the show, but also because of the necessity of getting the eye to certain places when the set is not doing that. The lights are proportionately more complicated than you would expect. The costumes are a fascinating deconstruction of colonial wear for the ensembles -

they're wearing the kind of things that refer to colonial ruffles and then they're wearing tights, modern looking. The principals are wearing these slightly electrified versions of costume, particularly the famous costume that Daveed Diggs wore when Jefferson shows up in the second act - brilliant purple, I'm not sure that Jefferson ever wore brilliant purple, but it's a brilliant theatrical moment.

Something else that's really interesting in the design of *Hamilton* is the sound. It doesn't get much attention, but it's perhaps the most non-naturalistic aspect of the production and is used in various special effects that are beautifully done. For instance, in the rewinding of the duels, you hear the sound of the of the dialogue that preceded it actually rewind and it helps to tell the story in a really prominent way. That's not so typical in musicals.

Both Kail and Miranda are steeped in the history of musical theatre, and the work of the artists who came before them. Although *Hamilton* has been repeatedly praised for its originality, its creator and director have acknowledged that a number of other shows had an important influence on their own production. Among what he called the 'grandparents' of *Hamilton*, Thomas Kail listed both *Sweeney Todd* and *Evita* as two productions that have had a clear impact on the staging of the show.

Michael Riedel: There are several influences on *Hamilton*, I think. Stephen Sondheim, as Lin acknowledges, because Steve wrote, of course, music and lyrics, but he also did adult shows, he didn't do musical fables, he didn't do shows for the tired businessmen, he did, with Hal Prince, challenging shows: *Company*, which is about marital strife; *Follies*, which is about ageing; and *Sweeney Todd*, which is about murder and cannibalism. So, he and Hal Prince, the great director, are important to *Hamilton* because they allowed musical theatre to deal with political, adult, contemporary, sometimes difficult themes; that musicals did not always have to end with happy people tap dancing.

I think the staging of *Sweeney Todd* is very important to the staging of *Hamilton* because it was on a grand scale with a lot of people that Hal was moving around, and you can see in Tom's staging of *Hamilton* echoes of Hal's original staging of *Sweeney Todd* because *Sweeney Todd* really evoked eighteenth-century London, right down to the fog coming off the Thames, much as the staging and the set design of *Hamilton* evokes those taverns lit by candlelight, where the Founding Fathers hashed out the country.

I would also say *1776* is a very important show that should not be overlooked. That was the first show written by Peter Stone, a show that said the Founding Fathers are not on Mount Rushmore, they're flesh and blood, vital human beings, they're petty, they're envious, they're funny, they squabble, they fight, they're also geniuses. Without *1776*, I don't think Lin could have pulled off *Hamilton*, he understood that Peter Stone found a way to make these historical figures individual people that a contemporary audience can respond to today, and that's what Lin does with *Hamilton*.

Jesse Green: There's certainly a lot of Evita in *Hamilton* in terms of a charismatic, central character who's a striver, but also the staging, the famous staging by Hal Prince, which was the beginning of the end of naturalistic staging in musicals. *Hamilton* takes over from that. There are no real "scenes", in *Hamilton*, it's all sung through or spoken through, and the material kind of emerges and steps back and emerges and steps back. All of this reminds me of *Evita*. Certainly, *Sweeney Todd* in the hugeness of the central character and the ambition of the work. The works of Kander and Ebb, *Chicago* and *Cabaret*, are certainly evident as an inspiration for the emphasis on thematic development in a show. I would also say, aside from the usual names you hear, Rodgers and Hammerstein are there - he quotes them subtly and humorously a lot. I think you can't forget Gilbert and Sullivan, also, the last real exemplars of that level of verbal wit in musical theatre as the main form of storytelling and the joy that that brings out. Even when it's unlike Gilbert and Sullivan, Lin-Manuel Miranda is using the fun of the rhymes, the internal rhymes, the rhythmic switches to make sure the audience is having an exciting and fun experience while they're absorbing a lot of material that may, in some cases, not be fun.

When, after *Hamilton's* opening Broadway run, the show was showered with awards, the achievement in staging was recognised, with David Korins, Andy Blankenbuehler, Paul Tazewell, Howard Binkley and, of course, Thomas Kail, all receiving Tony nominations.

Lin-Manuel Miranda: I started writing this in 2008, so this is a culmination of a lot of people putting a lot of hard work in, particularly Tommy Kail, who got all the artforms involved in making a musical and made them into one cohesive thing called *Hamilton*. And the fact that we have so many nominations is a celebration of how many art forms it takes to make a musical.

Given the scale of *Hamilton's* success, it became clear that Broadway would be too small to contain the show, and in 2016 the company had to start preparing for their musical to go global.

9. THE HAMILTON LEGACY

When *Hamilton* hit Broadway in the summer of 2015 it blew up, becoming nothing short of a phenomenon all over America. Amid the cascade of awards and critical praise, the show's success had seen it outgrow New York, and an expanded company prepared to bring Lin-Manuel Miranda's vision to the rest of the world.

Jesse Green: The critical reception for *Hamilton* was extraordinary. It was as if we poor few critics remaining in this world were just waiting for a chance to explode with happiness. You could argue it was a little overstated, but there really was

▲ *Hamilton at The Richard Rodgers Theater, W 46th St, Manhattan*

something there. Particularly when it opened at the Public Theater off-Broadway, the critics could respond to this work as something they found, which is never really true, but inflates the reaction to some degree. Most of the reviews spoke of the historic quality of the show.

The timing was really good. Television musicals and TV series that use singing are part of what paved the way for a greater popularity for the musical. Now, that said, there have been a number of hit musicals that reached out into the larger culture, like *Wicked*, but even they pale in comparison to what's going on with *Hamilton*. You still have to ask what is it about this material coming on top of those other things that was able to take advantage of the moment and reach out so far into the culture? And I think you have to go back to the medium, the use of hip-hop, which for the first time in musical theatre since possibly the '50s is a living form in popular music. For the last forty or fifty years, the way people sing in musicals, beautiful as it is, is not the same as what people are listening to on the radio or on their iPods. Now you have a musical that sounds a lot like what people, especially young people, are listening to. So that immediately provides access. The fact that it comes from an inclusive cast and a diverse group of creators takes the elitist stink off of musical theatre and also takes off the fear that this is going to be something fusty and irrelevant to real life, particularly if you think about somebody writing a show about *Hamilton* twenty-five years ago, you think, "Really? Who is that going to reach out to?" Lin-Manuel Miranda removed one-by-one all of the things that might keep people away from it. In a way, it has to do with what I have noticed about his personality, which is that he's a radical pleaser. And good for him if he can keep it up, that's amazing. But it's also very smart in terms of creating a business plan for a show.

Anthony DeCurtis: What often gets lost is the quality: it's really good, it's just *really good*. The socio-political aspects of it, the casting of it, all of that stuff, its connection to larger social issues now that are very much in the air concerning immigration and concerning race, that's obviously important, but if the play wasn't any good, the other stuff wouldn't have mattered.

As *Hamilton* prepared to move beyond New York, it took steps to embed the show's legacy, that had begun with its student outreach during the off-Broadway run, of a commitment to education, social justice, equality and opportunity for all.

In 2016 the Hamilton Education Program was founded with funding from the Rockefeller Foundation, it's stated goals are education, civic engagement, racial justice and gender equality. The program established the Ham4Progress Award for Educational Advancement, to support "college-bound high school students from communities that directly experience the consequences of injustice and discrimination" with tutoring, courses, college visits and learning technology.

Jason King: I think part of *Hamilton's* success is the fact that we're in New York and that Alexander Hamilton became a New York figure, and that it's hip-hop and hip-hop started in New York City. So there's this way in which the musical is a kind of commentary on New York itself and the power of New York. And that's certainly part of Lin-Manuel's work. *In The Heights* was a celebration of New York, and there's no reason to think that *Hamilton* itself is also not a celebration of New York. The fact that tickets were given out to students so that they could see it, I think was very heartening, it was a way to include students in the audience of *Hamilton* at a time in which the ticket prices would have been exorbitant.

▲   *Hamilton in Chicago*

Jayson Rodriguez: Lin-Manuel Miranda is a New Yorker, a Wesleyan graduate who likes *Star Wars* but also likes hip-hop - a unicorn, but not the only one. New York has this fabric that creates that, Lin-Manuel Miranda taps into that, the idea of what New York is. He's done this huge outreach to younger children, to make them be a part of this and go see matinees. That's great because they are him and he is them, and they are all this idea of New York. We're all drinking the same water of experience. Do I think *Hamilton* can emanate from any other part of the country? I don't think so.

In July 2016, Lin-Manuel gave a final, farewell performance as Alexander Hamilton, before his understudy Javier Muñoz stepped into the role. That fall, *Hamilton* embarked on its journey to becoming a global sensation. The play began a residence in Chicago, a touring cast was assembled to take the show around American cities, and it was announced that *Les Miserables* producer Cameron Mackintosh would put *Hamilton* on at the Victoria Palace Theatre in London, to be followed, starting in 2023, by a tour of the UK and Ireland.

In 2019 *Hamilton* opened in Puerto Rico, with Lin-Manuel Miranda himself returning to the stage to take the lead role in a moment of deep significance for the Miranda family. In 2021 the show premiered in Sydney, Australia, kicking-off an Australian tour that took in dates in Melbourne and Brisbane. In 2022 the first non-English language production of *Hamilton* opened in Hamburg, Germany and the first Asian show took place in Manila, Philippines, before moving on to Abu Dhabi and Singapore. For anyone unable to catch *Hamilton* live on stage, a filmed version was released in 2020 on Disney+. It has become, simply, one of the most successful musicals of all time.

Jason King: *Hamilton* has become such a huge phenomenon, largely because of Lin-Manuel Miranda. I think he's a genius. He's somebody who represents something that we haven't seen in the theatre in a long time: the self-contained auteur, who is really thoughtful about inclusion and issues of representation and diversity and who grabbed the brass ring and found a way to bring in a large cast of color to Broadway to tell a story about the founding of the nation in a way that's been very powerful. It's a show that is educational, it's entertaining, it's formally complex. It is also a show that is accessible enough that anybody could get into it, regardless of their relationship to American history.

▲ *The Miranda family at the unveiling of Lin's star on the Hollywood Walk of Fame*

Having stepped off the *Hamilton* stage Lin-Manuel Miranda quickly became a hugely sought-after artist and personality. He embarked on a long collaboration with Disney, contributing music to *Star Wars: The Force Awakens*, *Moana*, *Star Wars: The Rise of Skywalker*, *Encanto*, *The Little Mermaid* and *Mufasa: The Lion King*. He also landed a starring role in the Mary Poppins Sequel *Mary Poppins Returns*.

In 2021 a film adaptation of *In The Heights* was released to huge critical acclaim, and later that year Lin-Manuel made his big-screen debut as a director with *Tick, Tick…Boom!* Over the course of a decade since *Hamilton* first opened, Lin-Manuel Miranda has become one of the most famous names in America, celebrated by legions of fans, all of whom wait, with bated breath, to see what comes next from the man who re-awakened Broadway.

Michael Riedel: I think with a theater person, an artist like Lin-Manuel Miranda, you should expect the unexpected. His mind works in ways that mere mortals don't, he sees things that we don't. He read a nine-hundred-page biography of Alexander Hamilton, he saw a musical. He is like Andrew Lloyd Webber in that sense, Andrew read some nonsense poems for kids about cats and saw a musical. He's like Cameron Mackintosh, who picked up a thousand-page novel in French about a guy who steals bread and saw *Les Miserables*. He's like Michael Bennet, who thought the stories of the anonymous people that dance in the chorus can make their own show. I think theater people like that are going to come across something that captures their imagination that only they can see unfold in their head as a show and eventually they will create it on a stage for all of us to see and enjoy, so from Lin-Manuel Miranda, I expect something that I've never seen before.

As *Hamilton* approaches its 10-year anniversary, many of the questions that both the play and Alexander Hamilton, the historical figure, asked of America remain fiercely relevant. Issues around the constitution, separation of powers, the financial system, democracy and civil and minority rights have, if anything, become even more contested since the show first opened in New York. The topic of diversity and inclusion, on which *Hamilton*'s color-blind casting made such a powerful intervention, continues to be at the forefront of the national discourse.

It's now been long enough that a new generation will be able to discover *Hamilton* for the first time, engage with those questions and see American history in a new light. But, first and foremost, they will be able to be astonished, entertained and uplifted by a dazzling spectacle from a singular creative mind; as Anthony DeCurtis observed, *Hamilton* is *just really good*, and that, perhaps, is the most important message of all.

HAMILTON - PHOTO CREDITS

PICTURE CREDITS

Cover: The 58th Grammy Awards, *Hamilton* Performance. Theo Wargo/Getty Images.

Page 4: Lin Manuel-Miranda at the Tony Awards. Matteo Prandoni/Shutterstock

Page 12: In The Heights. Alastair Muir/Shutterstock

Page 15: Lin-Manuel Miranda at the 2019 San Diego Comic Con International. Gage Skidmore/Wikimedia Commons. CC BY-SA 2.0

Page 22: Alexander Hamilton by John Trumbull 1792. John Trumbull/Public domain via Wikimedia Commons

Page 24: Alexander Hamilton. John Trumbull, Public domain, via Wikimedia Commons

Page 28: Washington Constitutional Convention, 1787. Junius Brutus Stearns/Public domain via Wikimedia Commons

Page 30: Portrait of Aaron Burr, by John Vanderlyn 1802. John Vanderlyn/Public domain via Wikimedia Commons

Page 32: Alexander Hamilton & Aaron Burr prepare to duel. Weehawken, New Jersey, 1804. Public domain via Wikimedia Commons

Page 34: The Federalist Papers. Public domain via Wikimedia Commons

Page 35: Thomas Jefferson. Rembrandt Peale/Public domain via Wikimedia Commons

Page 35: James Madison. John Vanderlyn/Public domain via Wikimedia Commons

Page 39: Aaron Burr kills Alexander Hamilton. Weehawken, New Jersey, 1804. Public domain via Wikimedia Commons

Page 42: Lin Manuel Miranda, New York 2017. Kelly Taub/BFA/ Shutterstock

Page 43: The Cast of *Hamilton* at The White House, 2016. Amanda Lucidon/Public domain via Wikimedia Commons

Page 45: Lin Manuel Miranda in 2016. Comedy Central/Everett/ Shutterstock

Page 47: Oskar Eustis. Startraks/Shutterstock.

Page 48: Joe Papp. Gotfryd Bernard/Public domain via Wikimedia Commons

Page 50: The Public Theatre, Ajay Suresh from New York/Wikimedia Commons/CC BY 2.0

Page 54: *Hamilton* at The Richard Rodgers Theater, W 46th St, Manhattan. Andrew Cline/Shutterstock

Page 57: *A Chorus Line*. Andreas Praefcke/Wikimedia Commons/ CC BY 3.0

Page 58: Broadway, 2014. Alex Proimos/ /CC BY 2.0

Page 60: Rent. BroadwaySpain/ Wikimedia Commons/CC BY-SA 4.0

Page 62: Richard Rodgers Theater. Rblfmr/Shutterstock

Page 63: President Obama attends *Hamilton*, 2015. Pete Souza/Public domain via Wikimedia Commons

Page 65: Lin-Manuel Miranda as Alexander Hamilton. Steve Jurvetson/Wikimedia Commons/CC BY 2.0

Page 68: Lin-Manuel & the cast of *Hamilton*. Matt Baron/Shutterstock

Page 71: The cast of Hamilton in rehearsals, 2015. Carolyn Contino/ BEI/Shutterstock

Page 74: Leslie Odom Jr., Daveed Diggs and Renée Elise Goldsberry at the Tony Awards, 2016. Gregory Pace/Shutterstock

Page 83: The cast of Hamilton perform musical selections from *Hamilton*. Steve Jurvetson/Wikimedia Commons/CC BY 2.0

Page 85: Lin-Manuel Miranda. U.S. Department of the Treasury/ Public domain via Wikimedia Commons

Page 90:   Andy Blankenbuehler, Lin-Manuel Miranda, Alex Lacamoire
& Thomas Kail. Carolyn Contino/BEI/Shutterstock
Page 97:   Richard Rodgers Theater. Epicgenius/Wikimedia Commons/
CC BY-SA 4.0
Page 100: Hamilton at The Richard Rodgers Theater Paul Sableman/
Wikimedia Commons/CC BY 2.0
Page 102: The Miranda family at the unveiling of Lin's star on the
Hollywood Walk of Fame. Luke Harold/Wikimedia
Commons/CC0

QUOTATIONS

All quotations from Lin-Manuel Miranda, Daveed Diggs, Leslie Odom Jr., Renée Elise Goldberry and Thomas Kail taken from the documentary film *Hamilton: One Shot To Broadway* (Symettrica Entertainment Ltd, 2017) and are used under License.